Industrial Development in Mexico

This book explores developmental policymaking across the multiple levels of Mexico's contemporary state, arguing that many of the innovations in industrial policy have been driven at the subnational level. In the three decades since Mexico's neoliberal turn in its political economy, subnational units of government have taken a lead in industrial transformation, galvanising policy from below. With most literature on new developmentalism focusing on the national level, this book is an important exploration of the differentiated and rewarding results that may be found below the state's centre.

Based on an original dataset of written and oral interviews gained from national and subnational governmental units of industrial policymaking in Mexico, the book shows how attribution and power are diffused across the contemporary state's multiple levels. Notable subnational projects explored by the book include public-private collaboration, productive investments and an interesting array of incentives targeted towards industrial upgrading and innovation. The book concludes by providing a distinctive and systematic comparison between subnational units from different countries in Latin America and further afield, in order to assess the commonalities of developmental roles and policies.

Industrial Development in Mexico will be an important read for scholars across the fields of political science, political economy and Latin American development.

Walid Tijerina completed his doctoral studies at the University of York, UK, and now works at the Universidad Autónoma de Nuevo León, Mexico.

Routledge Studies in Latin American Development

The series features innovative and original research on Latin American development from scholars both within and outside of Latin America. It particularly promotes comparative and interdisciplinary research targeted at a global readership.

In terms of theory and method, rather than basing itself on any one orthodoxy, the series draws broadly on the tool kit of the social sciences in general, emphasizing comparison, the analysis of the structure and processes, and the application of qualitative and quantitative methods.

Market Liberalizations and Emigration from Latin America
Jon Jonakin

Money from the Government in Latin America
Conditional Cash Transfer Programs and Rural Lives
Edited by Maria Elisa Balen and Martin Fotta

Demobilisation and Reintegration in Colombia
Building State and Citizenship
Francy Carranza-Franco

Welfare and Social Protection in Contemporary Latin America
Edited by Gibrán Cruz-Martínez

Industrial Development in Mexico
Policy Transformation from Below
Walid Tijerina

Industrial Development in Mexico

Policy Transformation from Below

Walid Tijerina

LONDON AND NEW YORK

First published 2019
by Routledge
2 Park Square, Milton Park, Abingdon, Oxon OX14 4RN

and by Routledge
52 Vanderbilt Avenue, New York, NY 10017

Routledge is an imprint of the Taylor & Francis Group, an informa business

© 2019 Walid Tijerina

British Library Cataloguing-in-Publication Data
A catalogue record for this book is available from the British Library

Library of Congress Cataloging-in-Publication Data
A catalog record for this book has been requested

ISBN: 978-0-367-20946-9 (hbk)
ISBN: 978-0-429-26431-3 (ebk)

Typeset in Times New Roman
by Apex CoVantage, LLC

To the memory of my father

Contents

Tables

Acknowledgements

I owe special thanks to three universities which have supported the realisation of this research project that began back in 2014: the University of York, the Universidad Autónoma de Nuevo León (UANL) and the University of Texas at Austin. I am more than grateful to my mentors and colleagues at the political science departments in the University of York. Louise Haagh provided me with insightful guidance from this project's very start, and Carlos Solar has always been a stimulating interlocutor on Latin America's development. In the UANL, Abraham Hernández Paz has given me all the support a researcher could wish for. I want to express my gratitude as well to the University of Texas at Austin's LLILAS Benson Latin American Studies and Collection for sponsoring my research visit during the year 2016. Their vast library resources on Mexico and Latin America were of substantial use to my research, and the seminars, conferences and talks I attended gave me a rewarding opportunity to exchange ideas with their researchers, helping me clarify my own project.

Furthermore, I would like to give special thanks to two professors who kindly took time to review my project and provide feedback throughout several stages. Joel S. Migdal's invaluable feedback was key in shaping many of the theoretical and conceptual foundations of my research. Also, Diego Sánchez-Ancochea, from the Latin American Centre of the University of Oxford, provided sharp comments which helped me consolidate the project's analytical framework as well as encouraged me to pursue this project's publication as a book.

Regarding this book's editorial process, a special mention is due to Helena Hurd, whose guidance and support were filled with enthusiasm and helpful suggestions. I also wish to thank Leila Walker for all her support during the editorial process, and the constructive comments of two anonymous reviewers which helped me reshape this project for it to appeal to a wider audience.

Finally, I would like to thank my mother and brothers for giving me constant support throughout the duration of this endeavour. And, with a truly grateful mention, I want to thank my wife, Susana, for providing me with unending support, motivation and inspiration.

Abbreviations

ALTEX	Programme for Highly Exporting Enterprises
AMSDE	Mexican Association of Economic Development Secretaries
BDMG	Development Bank of Minas Gerais
CAINTRA	Chamber for the Transformative Industry (Mexico)
CDI	Company of Industrial Districts (Minas Gerais)
CECATI	Capacitation Centre for Industrial Labour (Querétaro)
CEMIG	Energy Company of Minas Gerais (Centras Elétricas de Minas Gerais)
CFE	Federal Commission of Electricity
CMIC	Mexican Chamber for the Construction Industry
CODIQUE	Committe for the Industrial Development of the State of Querétaro
COMEXQRO	Programme for Querétaro's International Commerce
CONACYT	National Council of Science and Technology
CONAGO	National Commission of Governors
COPARMEX	Confederation of Mexican Employers
EOS	export-oriented strategy
FDI	foreign direct investment
FICORCA	Exchange Risk Coverage Fund
GATT	General Agreement on Tariffs and Trade
ICA	Ingenieros Civiles Asociados
iNDEXTb	Industrial Extension Bureau (Gujarat)
INDI	Institute of Industrial Development (Minas Gerais)
ISI	import substitution industrialisation
MDDS	Most Different Design System
MIC	Ministry of Industry and Commerce
MITI	Ministry of International Trade and Industry (Japan)
MTYCIC	Monterrey, International City of Knowledge
NAFINSA	Nacional Financiera (Mexico's National Development Bank)
NAFTA	North American Free Trade Agreement

PAN	National Action Party
PEMEX	Petróleos Mexicanos
PIIT	Research and Technology Innovation Park (Nuevo León)
PITEX	Programme for Temporal Imports to Produce Exports
PRD	Party of the Democratic Revolution
PRI	Institutional Revolutionary Party
SAPs	structural adjustment packages
SEDEC	Secretariat of Economic Development (Nuevo León)
SEDESU	Secretariat of Sustainable Development (Querétaro)
SMEs	small and medium enterprises
SOE	State-Owned Enterprise
TNCs	transnational companies
Tremec	Transmisiones y Equipos Mecánicos
UANL	Autonomous University of Nuevo León
UdeM	University of Monterrey
UNAQ	National Aeronautic University at Querétaro

1 Introduction
Bringing the (developmental) state back in

Introduction

During the second half of the 20th century, East Asia and Latin America garnered attention at a global scale due to their similar trajectories of industrial development and high rates of GDP growth. During the 1980s, the projection of the "East Asian Miracle" led academics to start a research agenda with the objective of diagnosing the distinct characteristics and patterns that the Newly Industrialised Countries States exposed during their accelerated industrial transformation. Among several research studies, it was Chalmers Johnson's analysis (1982) on the Japanese Miracle and the central role of the Ministry of International Trade and Industry (MITI) in their country's rapid industrial transformation which seemed to better capture the role of the State in triggering this process.[1]

In the aforementioned study, MITI undertook a role of "administrative guidance" which not only provided direction, guidelines and encouragement to industries within a given strategic industry, but also retaliated and punished them with a wide range of actions, depending on each situation, with the ultimate goal of pursuing the country's industrial transformation. This administrative guidance was part of Johnson's (1982) broader concept of industrial policy, which entails "the activities of governments that are intended to develop or retrench various industries in a national economy in order to maintain global competitiveness" (p. 9).

A similar testimony of industrial policy implementation in pursuit of global competitiveness was later provided by Robert Wade's (1990) analysis of state-led development in Taiwan and Alice Amsden's (1992) account of Korean industrialisation, both of which emphasised state-society relations or public-private collaboration as key mechanisms that triggered economic development.

On the other side of the globe, Latin America had also formulated its own version of "national developmentalism", or *estado desenvolvimentista*, through sectorial industrial policies, protection of infant industries and a high ratio of public investment in infrastructure (see Bresser-Pereira, 1973). Nonetheless, Latin American States were often deemed as lacking the essential characteristics that the East Asian Tigers consolidated in their path towards successful industrialisation: centralisation of its developmental institutions, a meritocratic bureaucracy, and a long-term vision for a national industrialisation project (see Evans, 1995; Schneider, 1999).

By the 1980s, these two regions began to separate gradually with contrasting trajectories. The East Asian countries, led by Japan, South Korea and Taiwan, had successfully integrated their domestic industries into global productive chains of capital goods and high-tech manufactures, while the Latin American countries, exemplified mostly by Mexico and Brazil, extended their dependence on the export of commodities and on foreign technology.

A line of research thus began to be formulated in the pursuit of an explanation for Brazil and Mexico's developmental shortcomings. The failure of industrial upscaling suffered by these two countries was generally attributed to cronyism, rent-seeking, a lack of meritocracy and a reliance on import substitution industrialisation (ISI) strategies without an export-oriented strategy (EOS) (Evans, 1995; Schneider, 1999; Palma, 2009). However, the majority of these studies were based on either cross-national comparisons or individual case studies having nation-States as the sole unit of analysis, without giving further consideration to the multilevel intricacies inherent to large federal countries such as Brazil and Mexico.

Reconfiguring industrial policies for the new century

The incapacity of Latin American States to foster globally competitive industries at the end of the 20th century, along with successive financial crises, eventually led them to undertake a "neoliberal shift" in their economies. The market-oriented policies they implemented, however, did not provide the expected results. Most of the Latin American region underwent economic stagnation amid uncertainties about whether the market-oriented policies were to blame or whether the *manner* in which they were implemented was to blame. Debates aside, the extended stagnation in the region gave way to a resurgence of leftist political parties in Latin America.

This "pink tide" (Panizza, 2009) would eventually be a decisive element in the resurgence and reassessment of state-led policies of industrialisation. Within this context, Bresser-Pereira (2017) and Trubek (2013) detected particular sets of industrial policies in Brazil and Argentina which they conceptualised as a "new developmentalism" in the region. Straying away from traditional interventionist policies, this New Developmental State heightened instead public-private collaboration as a cornerstone for eliciting productive investments, technological innovation and export-oriented growth, along with an emphasis on a competitive exchange rate.

This reconfiguration of industrial policies in Latin America has thus far been cautious to mark its distance from the failures and bad reputation that State interventions generated after their shortfalls during the ISI period. Consequently, an effort has been made to put a new face on industrial strategies in the region by re-conceptualising them as "productive development policies" (see Melo & Rodríguez-Claré, 2006; Crespi, Fernández-Arias, & Stein, 2014), "new developmentalism" (Bresser-Pereira, 2017; Trubek, 2013) or "new industrial policy" (Devlin & Moguillansky, 2013). According to Moreno (2014), the "scope" of productive development policies "is the totality of the economy and not accelerated industrialization; their emphasis is competitiveness and integration with global value chains, not import substitution" p. xix, with a high reliance on the following policies: public-private collaboration, innovation, human capital improvement, clusters and internationalisation.

In Mexico, industrial policy too went from being "virtually banned from the official economic policy discourse" (Moreno-Brid, 2013, p. 226) to entering gradually the official discourse of President Peña Nieto's administration, including his National Development Plan 2012–2018. Three years into Peña Nieto's administration, however, industrial policies were already perceived more as static formulations of existing industries and quite limited to official discourse, without tangible impacts or results, which eventually led Mexican specialists on industrial policies to call, once again, for a "new industrial policy" (Sánchez & Moreno-Brid, 2016, p. 292).

Now, it is worth stressing that this reconfiguration of industrial policies based on public-private collaboration and innovation policies is not exclusive to the Latin American region or to developing countries. As Hausmann, Rodrik, and Sabel (2008) emphasised when extrapolating South Africa's recent industrialisation efforts onto the contemporary globalised conjuncture, "good" industrial policy is composed "of those institutional arrangements and practices that organize this (public-private) collaboration effectively" (p. 4). This public-private collaboration is now seen, throughout different States and international agencies, as one of the essential vehicles to achieve a more coordinated response to the evolving challenges that global productive chains demand, whether through subsidies, innovation policies, tax breaks, human capital improvement or quality standards, among others.

The approximation to industrial policy as being contingent on public-private collaboration that stresses innovation, human capital improvement, competitiveness, internationalisation and integration into global productive chains has been also detected in Nordic Europe. In their study, Ornston and Vail (2016) have shown how Finland had to reconfigure its industrial policies within a liberalised context, relying likewise on innovation policies, public-private collaboration and research and development (R&D) subsidies. This novel approach to industrial policy has begun to take hold in Latin America. In the words of Devlin and Moguillansky (2013), "new industrial policy (in the region) disassociates itself with government 'picking winners'. Rather governments should work with the private sector in search of opportunities and related obstacles to experimentation, learning and upgrading economic activities" (p. 17).

Overall, however, all of these lines of framework leave the more multileveled or fragmented characteristics of the developing world out of the picture. There thus seems to be a need "to disaggregate the state and to reorganize its units in a multilevel framework" (Sinha, 2003, p. 461). Though not in the developmental literature's mainstream, there have already been some case studies highlighting subnational efforts towards industrial transformation or, at least, case studies highlighting how subnational governments have found themselves in predicaments which pressured them, eventually, to devise their own responses to better position their economic development goals within both a national and a globalised context. Therefore, as the core chapters on Mexico's subnational strategies for industrialisation will highlight, there has been a consistent effort undertaken by subnational governments precisely through the policy mechanisms underscored by the literature on new industrial policy. To assess these testimonies of a new industrial policy in Mexican states, furthermore, the empirical chapters will build upon Naude's (2010) categorisation of industrial policy according to its domain and instruments.

In the first category, an industrial policy domain will denote areas of governmental activities covering a specific strategy – i.e. scientific innovation, selection of industrial sectors, improvement of technological capabilities and productivity strategies, among others. In the latter category, an industrial policy instrument will constitute the specific mechanism through which a government tries to attain its industrial objectives across the different domains – i.e. tax breaks, price regulations, exchange rate policy, incentives for foreign direct investment and promotion of public-private collaboration, among others.

The ultimate aim of this book is to provide a testimony of policy transformation at the subnational level from the Mexican perspective in order to contribute to a more multileveled comprehension of the developmental challenges prevailing in the developing world. It is worth noting, likewise, that the recent wave of nationalism across the globe, along with the demise of the Washington Consensus, has once again placed State-led strategies of development at the centre of both national and global agendas.

The global resurgence of protectionism: widening the policy space for developmentalism?

In the current state of matters regarding political economy at a global scale, there seem to be two main structural openings that the developmental policy regime could currently exploit: firstly, a resurgence of protectionist industrial policies across the globe, and secondly, a growing empowerment of subnational governments in their respective pursuits of economic development.

Since the global financial crisis of 2008, there has been a growing contestation of the neoliberal paradigm. This demotion of neoliberalism as the hegemonic paradigm in political economy for developed and developing countries alike has been increasingly associated with a global wave of disenchantment regarding policies of laissez-faire, austerity and openness: Brexit, Grexit, the rise of left wing parties in Spain and Portugal along with Donald Trump's protectionism, and the overall inroads of nationalism across the globe. It is against this backdrop that the literature of State-led development (Kohli, 2004; Schneider, 2015; Bresser-Pereira, 2017) has again asserted itself as a framework for the analysis of the current relationship between the State and an increasingly globalised market. Both developing and developed countries alike have therefore started to press again for the opening of their "policy spaces" (Rodrik, 2004; Khan, 2007) in their national and international agendas.

So instead of witnessing a complete State curtailment or an "eclipse of the state" (Evans, 1997) in policy areas related to economic development, the developmental roles have either restructured themselves within the new globalised context (Agosin, 2013; Mazzucato, 2015; Jessop, 2015) or diffused to subnational platforms (Schneider, 2015; Eaton, 2017). Furthermore, the growing citizen discontent regarding neoliberal paradigms has paved the way for the resurgence of a nationalist development agenda voiced by characters as dissimilar as the current US President (a multimillionaire from a rightist party) and the new President Elect in Mexico (a politician who thrives on principles of austerity from a leftist tradition). Therefore, the world seems to be going through yet another of Polanyi's (1944) diagnosed "double movements" in relation to political economy preferences across the globe.

In a quite insightful work on the presence of multilevel governance and ideology conflicts in Andean countries, Eaton (2017) has highlighted how the back and forth shifts of States between market-centred and state-centred models of political economy give a "strong sense of déjà vu" p. 2. This oscillatory characteristic of political economy preferences at a global scale has a particular resonance with Polanyi's (1944) articulation of the "double movement", where intermittent failures of a chosen model (market-centred or state-centred) lead eventually to a replacement of the economic development model by its counterpart.

In the particular case of Latin America, these oscillatory shifts between economic development models have generally been more radical than in other regions due to the almost cyclical appearance of *fracasomanías*: a "failure complex" which has constantly led Latin American States to go back and forth, rather radically, between policy regimes at the first contact with resistance or failure (e.g. the abandonment of ISI models during the latter and more complex stages of industrial upgrading) (see Hirschman, 1975).

One of the complementing arguments of this work is that the current interscalar reconfiguration of States has led to a previously unwitnessed overlap of double movements in economic development policy regimes. Prior to the conjuncture of globalisation, democratisation and decentralisation (what I will call a "multilevel conjuncture" throughout the following chapters), the double movement in a State's political economy had a unitary articulation at a national scale. In this sense, Mexico or Brazil as a whole went back and forth between market-centred and state-centred models covering their nation's territory. The regional variation of success in these countries, which will be highlighted in chapter 3, depended on the disparate subnational capacities of integration and institutionalisation, but there was no policy regime contradiction between State levels. In contrast, after the multilevel conjuncture that has taken shape since the end of the 20th century, Mexico has kept intensifying its commitment to neoliberal capitalism at a national level, whilst having a double movement or contradictory policy regime from below in several of its states.

It is worth highlighting that Brazil and Mexico could again enter into contrasting policy regimes at the national level, as far-right presidential candidate Bolsonaro won Brazil's presidential election by voicing support for an open market economy, numerous privatisations and measures of fiscal austerity. Up until several years ago, Bolsonaro had praised the national industrialisation system of Brazil's military regime, but the appearance of Paulo Guedes as his economic adviser (a banker with a Ph.D. from the University of Chicago) has represented a radical shift in his political economy position, in an apparent effort to exploit the *anti-petista* movement – the movement against Lula da Silva's Partido dos Trabalhadores. Therefore, if Bolsonaro deepens President Temer's commitment to a market-oriented model, there is a high probability that subnational governments will devise or continue to strengthen their more statist development models, eventually echoing the interscalar incompatibilities to be explored in the empirical chapters.

These multileveled dynamics will hopefully complement and extend the growing literature on Latin America's subnational politics, particularly with Gibson's (2005) "political regime juxtaposition" and Eaton's (2017) "policy regime juxtaposition". Throughout this book, nonetheless, my approach will deviate somewhat from Eaton's assessment of the aforementioned juxtaposition as "subnational contestation" or "subnational policy challenge". Rather, my approach regarding interscalar incompatibility will stress the importance of vertical integration between national and subnational levels of government as a contributing factor to achieving industrial transformation, *even though* there was a contradictory policy regime – hence the importance this book confers to more multileveled characteristics of Latin America's development.

At the same time, this body of research represents an effort to set the analytical bases for examining the upcoming impacts that yet another shift towards a state-centred model will have on ongoing developmental efforts from below. With an apparent return to more developmental or *desarrollista* approaches at the national level in Mexico's new President Elect's agenda, there could once again be an interscalar developmental compatibility, which, as the chapter on Mexico's ISI will demonstrate, has been vital to further the opportunities of subnational industrialisation.

Overview of the book

In pursuit of the objectives presented in the previous sections, the book is structured as follows. The following chapter will explore the rather scattered testimonies of industrialisation or developmental efforts conducted by subnational governments. It will thus remark that the conjuncture of globalisation, democratisation and decentralisation during the previous decades has increasingly diffused power and attributions throughout the different levels of the State. This has led to a reassessment of the analytical perspectives necessary for the study of the State based on elements of space, geography and international political economy. How, then, has this state reconfiguration impacted developing countries' industrialisation projects? This chapter will argue that this diffusion of state attributions has been even more acute in the developing world, where States have traditionally failed in consolidating an effective centre. Furthermore, the chapter will argue that this lack of an effective centre in the developing world led, even before the globalisation-democratisation conjuncture, to more multileveled dynamics of development.

Then, the book's third chapter will first present a multileveled assessment of Mexico's industrial development: a case study of a Mexican state located in the central region called the Bajío. This chapter will highlight how a subnational unit in Mexico embraced a proactive role in upgrading its industrial landscape by integrating or inserting itself into the nationwide efforts of industrialisation during the country's ISI period. Moreover, it will translate the Gerschenkronian literature on "backward states" and "catching-up" industrial strategies to Mexico's fragmented context considering that, during the 1950s, Querétaro was still one of the most impoverished Mexican states with a prevailing rural landscape.

The question that the following chapters will explore is what happens to a developing country's subnational development when its national government embraces market-oriented reforms? Since the 1980s, Mexico has embraced a neoliberal turn in its political economy, shifting radically from a closed economy with high State intervention to an open economy with decreasing State intervention. However, the ongoing market-oriented policies generated various responses at the subnational level. These empirical chapters (chapters 4 and 5) are supported on a subnational comparative method in order to assess the developmental role that two subnational units have consolidated in contrast to the non-interventionist stance of the federal government. One of the first effects that globalisation and the North American Free Trade Agreement (NAFTA) had on Mexican industrialised states was the displacement of domestic industries amid increasing international competition (Peters, 2000). Therefore, through a Most Different Design System of comparison, I highlight how two contrasting Mexican states relied on similar developmental policies and institutions to regain their industrial competitiveness in the new globalised context.

Despite the substantive differences between Nuevo León and Querétaro regarding geography, political composition, population and timing of their industrialisations, they both achieved a transformation from a rural to an industrial economy and later, in a globalised context, an industrial scaling-up from mid- or low-technology manufactures to high-technology manufactures with a local integration that surpasses the average deficiencies of the "subcontracting" (Bizberg, 2018) or *maquila* model of Mexico's export sector. This section will thus consolidate the assessment of the variables or factors which contributed to an industrial transformation from below in the Mexican context. As will be detailed, the success of the developmental or *desarrollista* policies at a subnational level in both Nuevo León and Querétaro included a twofold strategy: firstly, an element of vertical integration within Mexico's different levels of government, and secondly, a horizontal strategy of institutionalisation with an emphasis on state-society collaboration.

After analysing those two testimonies of subnational industrialisation in Mexico, the following chapter will extrapolate the cited factors and comparative insights to subnational efforts undertaken in Latin America and beyond. Consequently, this comparative chapter will build on the discussion set up in previous chapters. It seeks to extrapolate Mexico's experiences to two other developing countries: Brazil and India. This chapter will therefore look to underscore how, amid differentiated economic and democratic transitions, subnational units of government deployed multileveled strategies of industrialisation to trigger their economic development. Furthermore, the present chapter will present a brief overview of "failed" or "negative cases" in Mexico, Brazil, Peru and India, to explore the outcomes of subnational industrialisation efforts when there is either an absence of a vertical integration with federal or central governments, or a lack of horizontal institutionalisation.

Finally, the concluding section will return to the central questions put forward since the initial chapters: How can subnational industrialisation efforts be assessed within the developing world? What have been the implications of the ongoing State reconfigurations for developmental efforts? And, lastly, are these testimonies or lessons transferrable to other developing contexts? Overall, the final chapter will summarize the findings and insights provided by the case studies in an effort to distil the main variables that have been present in industrial transformations led by subnational governments, along with other comparative insights which might be translated to research on subnational politics not exclusive to the political economy realm. In particular, what I have termed "interscalar incompatibility or compatibility" will hopefully resonate with the democratisation literature on juxtaposition of political regimes across a State's different levels (see Gibson, 2005; Giraudy, 2013) and the juxtaposition of policy regimes within the Andean countries of Latin America (see Eaton, 2017).

Note

1 Throughout the book, "nation-States" will be referred to as "States" with an initial capital, in order to distinguish them from subnational states ("states") which form part of the intermediate level of government.

References

Agosin, M. R. (2013). *Productive development policies in Latin America: Past and present*. Santiago: University of Chile, Department of Economics.

Amsden, A. (1992). *Asia's next giant: South Korea and late industrialization*. Oxford: Oxford University Press.

Bizberg, I. (2018). Varieties of capitalism, growth and redistribution in Asia and Latin America. *Brazilian Journal of Political Economy*, *38*(2), 261–279.

Bresser-Pereira, L. C. (1973). O novo modelo brasileiro de desenvolvimento, *Revista Dados*, *11*, 122–145.

Bresser-Pereira, L. C. (2017). Two forms of capitalism: Developmentalism and economic liberalism. *Brazilian Journal of Political Economy, 37*(4), 680–703.

Crespi, G., Fernández-Arias, E., & Stein, E. (Eds.). (2014). *Rethinking productive development.* New York, NY: Palgrave Macmillan.

Devlin, R., & Moguillansky, G. (2013). *What's new in the new industrial policy in Latin America?* Policy Research Working Paper. Washington, DC: World Bank.

Eaton, K. (2017). *Territory and ideology in Latin America: Policy conflicts between national and subnational governments.* Oxford: Oxford University Press.

Evans, P. (1995). *Embedded autonomy: States and industrial transformation/ Embedded autonomy.* Princeton, NJ: Princeton University Press.

Evans, P. (1997). The eclipse of the state? Reflections on stateness in an era of globalization. *World Politics, 50*(1), 62–87.

Gibson, E. (2005). Boundary control: Subnational authoritarianism in democratic countries. *World Politics, 58*(1), 101–132. Retrieved from www.jstor.org/ stable/40060126

Giraudy, A. (2013). Varieties of subnational undemocratic regimes: Evidence from Argentina and Mexico. *Studies in Comparative International Development, 48*(1), 51–80.

Hall, P. A., & Soskice, D. (Eds.). (2001). *Varieties of capitalism: The institutional foundations of comparative advantage.* Oxford: Oxford University Press.

Hausmann, R., Rodrik, D., & Sabel, C. (2008). *Reconfiguring industrial policy: A framework with an application to South Africa.* Working paper. Cambridge, MA: John F. Kennedy School of Government.

Hirschman, A. O. (1975). Policymaking and policy analysis in Latin America—a return journey. *Policy Sciences*, 6(4), 385–402.

Jessop, B. (2015). *The state: Past, present, future.* London: John Wiley & Sons.

Johnson, C. (1982). *MITI and the Japanese miracle: The growth of industrial policy: 1925–1975.* Stanford, CA: Stanford University Press.

Khan, S. R. (2007). WTO, IMF and the closing of development policy space for low-income countries: A call for neo-developmentalism. *Third World Quarterly*, 1073–1090.

Kohli, A. (2004). *State-directed development: Political power and industrialization in the global periphery.* Cambridge: Cambridge University Press.

Mazzucato, M. (2015). *The entrepreneurial state: Debunking public vs. private sector myths.* New York, NY: Anthem Press.

Melo, A., & Rodríguez-Clare, A. (2006). *Productive development policies and supporting institutions in Latin America and the Caribbean.* Washington, DC: Inter-American Development Bank.

Moreno, L. A. (2014). Preface. In G. Crespi, E. Fernández-Arias, & E. Stein (Eds.), *Rethinking productive development.* New York, NY: Palgrave Macmillan.

Moreno-Brid, J. C. (2013). Industrial policy: A missing link in Mexico's quest for export-led growth. *Latin American Policy, 4*(2), 216–237.

Naudé, W. (2010). *Industrial policy: Old and new issues (No. 2010, 106).* Working paper//World Institute for Development Economics Research.

Ornston, D., & Vail, M. I. (2016). The developmental state in developed societies: Power, partnership, and divergent patterns of intervention in France and Finland. *Comparative Politics, 49*(1), 1–21.

Palma, J. G. (2009). Flying-geese and waddling-ducks: The different capabilities of East Asia and Latin America to 'demand-adapt' and 'supply-upgrade' their export productive capacity. *Industrial Policy in Developing Countries*. Oxford: Oxford University Press.

Panizza, F. (2009). *Contemporary Latin America: Development and democracy beyond the Washington consensus*. London: Zed Books Ltd.

Peters, E. D. (2000). *Polarizing Mexico: The impact of liberalization strategy*. Boulder, CO: Lynne Rienner Publishers.

Polanyi, K. (1944). *The great transformation: Economic and political origins of our time*. New York, NY: Farrar & Rinehart.

Rodrik, D. (2004). *Industrial policy for the twenty-first century (No. 4767)*. CEPR Discussion Papers.

Sánchez, I. L., & Moreno-Brid, J. C. (2016). El reto del crecimiento económico en México: industrias manufactureras y política industrial. *Revista finanzas y política económica, 8*(2), 271–299.

Schneider, B. R. (1999). The Desarrollista state in Brazil and Mexico. In M. Woo-Cummings (Ed.), *The developmental state* (pp. 276–305). Ithaca, NY: Cornell University Press.

Schneider, B. R. (2015). *Designing industrial policy in Latin America: Business-state relations and the new developmentalism*. New York, NY: Springer.

Sinha, A. (2003). Rethinking the developmental state model: Divided leviathan and subnational comparisons in India. *Comparative Politics*, 459–476.

Trubek, D. M. (2013). Law, state, and the new developmentalism. An introduction. In D. Trubek et al. (Eds.), *Law and the new developmental state: The Brazilian experience in Latin American context* (pp. 1–27). Cambridge: Cambridge University Press.

Wade, R. (1990). *Governing the market: Economic theory and the role of government in East Asian industrialization*. Princeton, NJ: Princeton University Press.

2 Multilevel industrialisation in the developing world

Introduction

A conjuncture of globalisation and democratisation during the previous decades has increasingly diffused power and attributions throughout the different levels of the State. This has led to a reassessment of the analytical perspectives necessary for the study of the State based on elements of territory, geography, intergovernmental relations and international political economy. How, then, has this State reconfiguration impacted developing countries' industrialisation projects? One of the central aims of this book is precisely to explore developmental policymaking following the ever growing diffusion of attributions and power across the contemporary state's multiple levels, highlighting how the more multileveled nuances of the state have put to the test the current orthodoxies for promoting economic development at a national scale either through statist or neoliberal dictums.

In Charles Tilly's (1975) classic regarding the formation of states in Europe during the 16th and 17th centuries, the ability of a State to centralise its organisational capacities proved to be central to its probabilities of survival. The formation of a State with stability and managerial efficiency demanded that its government be able to centralise its functions, in opposition to the fragile city-states portrayed by Machiavelli or the "warring states" prior to the first great Chinese dynasties. In a sort of positive feedback, the increasing military sophistication that States required amid constant conflicts demanded, in turn, an increase of economic resources in order to finance a permanent army. The unity of the States since the 16th century became, therefore, fundamental to the consolidation of the security of the State from its borders outward.

In the case of the industrialisation of late developing countries during the previous century, the autonomy of the State and its capacity for centralisation played a similar role. At that time, both Asian and Latin American governments came to the conclusion that industrialisation was necessary to be on par with the world powers. In this tenor of ideas, the developmental governments of the East Asian Tigers reached the conclusion that to transform the national industry, the whole country needed to share the same objectives. And to make sure they were all on the same page, their governments deployed substantial bureaucratic efforts and resources to penetrate their society across the totality of their jurisdiction (see Kohli, 2004).

In Japan, as Chalmers Johnson's (1982) study portrays, this was done through a "developmental consensus" at the national level. The government took advantage of external threats and the need to be militarily self-sufficient to get the support of the entire population in building the country's domestic industries – a motivation that has been generally seen in the majority of successful industrial transformations (e.g. the Blue Water strategy in the United Kingdom) (Weiss & Hobson, 1995). As a result, the Ministry of International Trade and Investment (MITI) had the possibility of establishing an accelerated industrialisation as a unified national goal – along with its considerable sacrifices.

The advent of globalisation and democratisation trends since the end of the 20th century, however, has augmented the challenges that the modern State had sorted out in regards to its policymaking attributions. In Jessop's (2015) perspective, during the Fordist post-war period, the national state was "the primary scale of political organization", but now, "the current post-Fordist period is marked by the dispersion of political and policy issues across different scales of organization" (p. 144). Now, to better analyse the interscalar or multilevel dimensions of developmentalism, the first step is to identify which unit of analysis has been the main receptor of the diffusion of state power and state strategies regarding economic development. In India's case, for instance, Sinha (2005) remarks how "the levers of political authority vis-à-vis economic policy are located at the provincial level in India" (p. 463).

After reviewing the literature on Latin America's decentralisation of economic policymaking, we can similarly find that the governmental level that has been the main recipient of devolved attributions is the intermediate or subnational level (Eaton, 2017, 2004; Wilson, Ward, Spink, & Rodriguez, 2008; Montero, 2002). Thus, following the advent of globalisation and democratisation trends across the globe, subnational governments have taken a more proactive role in advancing their state's development opportunities through a varied array of industrial policies.

This chapter will argue that this diffusion of state attributions has been even more acute in the developing world, where states have traditionally failed in consolidating an effective centre. Furthermore, the chapter will argue that this lack of an effective centre in the developing world led, even before the globalisation-democratisation conjuncture, to more multileveled dynamics of development.

The state in the developing world and its interscalar reconfiguration

In Latin America, along with big countries such as India and China, this centralising capacity has always proved to be a major challenge to any national project of industrial transformation due to the existence of a considerably higher population, more extensive territories and multiple social cleavages. As related by Shils (1975), the "Third World" seldom exhibited an effective centre, let alone an effective developmental centre; one reason why a more multileveled approach underscores the importance of the periphery and periphery feedbacks in regards to the Third World. Consequently, through this perspective, the State becomes disentangled not only from its more unitary approaches of autonomy, but also from its unitary centre. In a country where the State is incapable of centralising control, the multiple feedbacks generated from the periphery or from below gain further relevance. And these are feedbacks which, in turn, have seldom been portrayed in industrialisation processes across the developing world.

Furthermore, on a related note, it is worth stressing how Latin American States have frequently struggled to strike a balance between centralisation and decentralisation of governmental attributions. Decentralisation was undertaken in a more systemic manner at the end of the 20th century in Latin America's "third wave of democratisation", but the region had already experimented widely with the devolution of authority in preceding decades. As highlighted by Eaton (2004), statism did not always translate to centralisation in the Latin American region prior to its third wave of democratisation. There have been testimonies in Brazil, Argentina and Uruguay in which statism and the prerogative of economic development throughout the ISI period were supported on the "expansion" of subnational authority (Eaton, 2004, p. 36), due precisely to the varying social and political cleavages of the region.

After the third wave of democratisation, however, the Latin American region did undergo an acute political reconfiguration, as it has also witnessed a diffusion of authority across different governmental levels that does not necessarily involve a formal or political process of decentralisation. Thus, with the recent multilevel conjuncture of globalisation, democratisation and decentralisation across the globe, the challenge of centralising economic development has been intensified even more due to "deterritorializing" and "destatizing" dynamics of the State (Jessop, 2015). Since 2004, and in parallel with the increasing impact of globalisation on the modern state, Brenner (2004) provided a reassessment of the analytical perspectives necessary for the study of the State based on elements of space, geography and international political economy. In the current globalised context, these "structural configurations" of contemporary States have reinforced an issue that Brenner (2004) considered central: uneven spatial development. This reinforcement of an uneven development within national contexts has been even more acute in Third World States, where the centre, as the hierarchical governmental unit, has had a troublesome path towards consolidation (see Shils, 1975; Migdal, 2001).

These uneven and galvanised characteristics of States in the developing world have thus far generated insightful contributions to the literature on democratisation, highlighting the manner in which contrasting political regimes (e.g. democratic vs authoritarian) might overlap across State levels in Latin America (see Gibson, 2005). Gradually, these more fragmented perspectives of Latin American States set the table for analytical frameworks on Latin American development that go well beyond the State centre. Susan Gauss (2010), for instance, underscores how Mexico's regional disparities and the varying power of regional elites fragmented the State's nationwide project of industrial transformation into an increasingly uneven development. This account has resonated with Montero's (2002) analysis of "shifting states" in Brazil, which relates the impact that Brazil's "asymmetrical federalism" had in generating differentiated development strategies and results at a subnational scale.

The varied impact that these spatial inequalities have on development has thus been analysed in countries such as China (Yang, 2018), India (Sinha, 2003, 2005), Brazil (Montero, 2002) and Mexico (Hiskey, 2005; Snyder, 2001a). Furthermore, not only have these same studies "scaled down" (Snyder, 2001b) the units of analysis to better comprehend the new scalar dimensions of development, but they have also highlighted the protagonist role that provincial, intermediate or subnational governments have displayed in pursuit of economic development in their particular jurisdictions. So, how could this multilevel dynamics contribute to a better understanding of new developmental policy regimes? And how could a comparative approach contribute in assimilating the interscalar or multilevel interactions of contemporary States?

This prevalent research lacuna in the developmental literature represents therefore the opportunity of translating the current circumstances of new developmental testimonies to a structural conjuncture in which the Westphalian dictum of State unity no longer holds true. It is necessary to remark that subnational or provincial governments are generally constrained from implementing the traditional macroeconomic developmental policies which are exclusive to federal or central governments (e.g. a competitive exchange rate or protectionist tariffs), but subnational governments are still appropriating the role of developmental promoters and policymakers within their jurisdictional limits with transcending results.

The diffusion of developmental attributions: mapping subnational strategies across the globe

Prior to the trade liberalisation period in the Latin American region, and witnessed mostly from the 1930s to the 1980s, subnational governments in Brazil and Mexico embraced developmental responsibilities generally within two scenarios: in the first scenario, national governments relied upon lower levels as a method of compensating for the lack of centralising capacities, expanding in the meantime the developmental institutions and responsibilities of subnational governments (see Eaton, 2004; Montero, 2002); and, in the second scenario, subnational governors worked as power-brokers to try to insert their jurisdiction's developing efforts and interests into a national project of industrial transformation, in some cases in spite of path-dependent policies which had generally excluded less developed provinces (as chapter 3 will examine through the analysis of Querétaro).

In both cases, however, there is an ongoing process of policy transformation from below in which subnational governments exploit the "policy windows" (Sætren, 2016) left open by national governments' development models, until elaborating their very own policy regime – or, more particularly, their very own *developmental* policy regime. During Latin America's ISI period, the policy transformations weaved from below followed the same developmental orientation designed at the national level, with an emphasis on import substitution, industrialisation and infrastructural upgrading. This "integrationist" relation between subnational and national development plans was generally constrained by the inherent characteristics of authoritarian governments prior to democratic transitions, as has been reviewed by Sinha (2005) for the cases of authoritarian Brazil, the former Soviet Union and 20th-century China. However, it is only after the trade liberalisation period undertaken in the Latin American region that there has been increasing space for dissent regarding economic development models, due in large part to the recent political and economic dynamics which have accentuated a diffusion of authority across governmental levels.

This downward diffusion of attributions and resources across a State because of democratisation and economic opening has been illuminatingly portrayed by Montero (2002) for the cases of Spain and Brazil during the 1970s and 1980s. According to Montero (2002), the implementation of both democratisation and liberal structural reforms in these countries "encouraged decentralization of authorities and resources once controlled by the central government", which in turn motivated subnational governments to exploit these newfound resources in order to formulate their own industrial policies as a response to economic crises and challenges (p. 42).

And although the decentralisation of attributions and resources has given subnational governments a greater opportunity to respond to contemporary challenges with major promptness and contextualisation, this devolution has also brought its own perils, particularly in the case of Latin America. Throughout the previous century, Brazil's periods of accentuated fiscal decentralisation led shortly afterwards to debt crises among Brazilian states. In Brazil, the unprecedented decentralisation of fiscal resources through the 1988 constitution contributed to severe fiscal crises across numerous states. In the words of Dillinger, Perry, and Webb (1999), the absence of "hard budget constraints for (Brazilian) states" led to Brazil's primary macroeconomic crisis after the third wave of democratisation: "excessive state deficits and then the mismanagement of the debt" (pp. 94–95).

During the first decade of the 21st century, Mexico too devolved fiscal resources extensively whilst removing many of the hard budget constraints on Mexican states' financial management, which eventually led to a high indebtedness at the subnational level. By the first quarter of 2015, the balance of the debt of the states and municipalities as a whole amounted to 510,030.8 million pesos, representing a real growth of 343% between 1993 and 2015 (IMCO, 2015). This exponential growth of subnational debts in Mexico is reflected, likewise, in the growth of the average debt as a percentage of a state's GDP. Mexican states like Chihuahua and Quintana Roo had an average of 8.18% and 7% in the second quarter of 2016, respectively, considerably higher than the 2% average of Mexican states during the 1990s (see IMCO, 2016; Dillinger et al., 1999).

Still, given the constraints or dependency that subnational governments experience with regards to national governments, one of my corollary arguments is that the national government will always play a key role in the success or failure of subnational strategies of development, whether through the formal decentralisation of resources, the informal distribution of financial or infrastructural resources or, more simply, access to information – be it development plans, priorities or technical information. It is thus in this particular aspect that my research on Mexico finds parallel scenarios of national-subnational interactions during the conformation of developmental projects from below in other countries such as Brazil, Spain, China and India. Thus, the first independent variable that I have detected in successful subnational strategies is what I term "vertical integration", which stresses the importance of centre-local dynamics in governmental relations.

Within the empirical chapters, therefore, I will highlight how subnational governments' strategies to access either national resources or developmental priorities seemed to be a prerequisite for the eventual success of their subnational industrialisation projects. Consequently, this book will keep in mind the relevance that each governmental level has across a State, and even more within federal regimes such as those analysed in both the empirical and the comparative chapters. Testimonies of other subnational strategies from provinces as disparate as Minas Gerais in Brazil and Gujarat in India have shown how their development has been contingent not only on the policies and strategies formulated by their governors and societal actors, but also on the policies and resources found at the national level. It is in these scenarios, then, that variables of political party conformation and intergovernmental relations come into play in varying ways.

After the prerequisite of vertical integration has crystallised, it is the horizontal strategies that a subnational government deploys within its jurisdiction which become essential in enhancing its developmental trajectories. The horizontal institutionalisation of developmental policies will consequently be considered as the other independent variable, along with strategies of vertical integration. As reviewed in the wider literature, among both developed and developing countries (Weiss & Hobson, 1995, pp. 230–244), industrial transformations across the globe have relied on a virtuous alliance between state and society. It is the existence of this element within the formulas for rapid industrialisation that led Peter Evans (1995) to formulate his concept of "embedded autonomy", cited in previous chapters.

More recently, Schneider (2015) and Hausmann, Rodrik, and Sabel (2008) have also underscored the importance of setting up the correct institutions for the enhancement of public-private collaboration within Latin America and South Africa, respectively. Thus, in this particular axis of my analytical framework, I will be reviewing the role that public-private institutions played in formulating and maintaining policy mechanisms which elicited developmental outcomes. In this case, the developmental outcome or dependent variable assessed throughout the case studies is an industrial transformation evidenced either in the construction of a comparative industrial advantage or in a transition to higher technological sectors as a response to national and international challenges.

From here on, likewise, this book will stress the importance of casting aside the "developmental State" as a historically contingent organisational complex. Rather, the arguments undertaken throughout the following chapters will underscore the importance of developmentalism as a "policy regime" (see Eaton, 2017) and an alternative to the recently hegemonic model of neoliberal capitalism (see Bresser-Pereira, 2017). In this order of ideas, the book works with the definition of policy regime provided by May and Jochim (2013, pp. 427–428) as a "governing arrangement" consisting of three essential elements: a central idea, institutional arrangements and interests which represent the bases of support or opposition.

Now, in what I have considered a developmental policy regime in the present work, the essential characteristics of the developmental state according to Doner, Ritchie, and Slater (2005) are present. Even at a subnational level and within the more *desarrollista* constraints of Mexico, the subnational governments of Nuevo León and Querétaro endeavoured to constitute themselves as "organizational complexes in which expert and coherent bureaucratic agencies collaborate with organized private sector to spur (sub)national growth" (Doner et al., 2005, p. 328) through sectorial policies emphasising local industrial upgrading, import substitution and integration of local firms into global productive chains. These policy mechanisms will accordingly resonate with the new developmental or the productive development policies described in the previous chapter.

Industrial development in Mexico: once fragmented, always fragmented?

The Mexican state has historically failed to develop a coordinated and cohesive developmental centre. Owing perhaps to the influence of successful developmental cases and their academic examinations (Johnson, 1982; Wade, 1990; Amsden, 1992), studies on Mexico (Schneider, 1999; Bennett & Sharpe, 1982; Moreno-Brid & Ros, 2009) have relied on the same centre-based approach in an effort to illustrate the country's industrialisation process. The benchmark for comparison has thus generally been Korea, Japan or Taiwan, which proved to have a successful developmental centre through MITI, the Economic Planning Board and a handful of central agencies with shared roles, respectively; however, Mexico's industrialisation has not exhibited the same capabilities.

To address this puzzle and the central questions posed above, this work will analyse the patterns and variables that were present in Mexican states which managed to achieve industrial transformations in different timeframes: firstly, within a context of national developmentalism based on ISI, and secondly, within a globalised context in which the national government had very much withdrawn from state-led development and vertical industrial policies.

In other words, in the case of Mexico's industrialisation, its incapacity to consolidate an efficient developmental centre led to a multiplication of the arenas in which industrial policies were to be set. Fieldwork in several Mexican states, consisting mainly of elite semi-structured interviews and the gathering of information from documentary sources, provided testimony of how the periphery had historically played an important role in the country's industrialisation. There was not only subnational variation in industrialisation processes across Mexico, but also a *subnational transformation*. Mexico's several stages and projects of industrial transformation were therefore constructed through various sets of policies at different State levels (national and subnational). Consequently, as stated by Migdal (2001), the periphery became "far more important in shaping the future of society" (p. 54) than the more traditional centre-focused studies generally admit.

Through fieldwork conducted in Mexico since 2014, it became evident that due to the fragmentation of the Mexican State, the industrial transformation was constructed in a polyphony that navigated through the different levels of the State. Furthermore, the initial findings of my research also suggested that it was at the subnational level, and not the federal level, that the institutionalisation of state-society relations, an "embedded autonomy" (Evans, 1995) or a "horizontal embeddedness" (Montero, 2002) had a better chance of flourishing.

This juncture in the research process led me to reconsider the capacities of the Mexican State and its particular (and fragmented) political development to postulate, as a result, the main argument of this work: that the public-private synergies needed for industrial transformation in Mexico were better formulated at the subnational level, and not at the federal or national level. As a result, this book will argue, these synergies gave way to parallel patterns of industrial policy and public-private relations in both Nuevo León and Querétaro that contributed to the culmination of an industrial transformation.

The present book thus aims to expand the studies on the industrialisation of Mexico through two main approaches. In the first place, by adopting a historical institutional approach to the industrialisation of Mexico, it intends to relate the evolution of an institutional system of industrial policy over time. Secondly, it aims to give testimony to the more multileveled characteristics of successful industrial transformations in Mexico, with a particular focus on the interactions between subnational governments and the federal government.

Afterwards, the subnational testimonies from Mexico's industrial development will be translated to other cases of subnational industrialisation in Latin America and beyond, looking to distil the patterns and variables that have enhanced an industrial transformation from below. As will be argued in both the theoretical and empirical chapters, the fragmented characteristics of States in the developing world have often been overshadowed in the literature of industrialisation and developmentalism by extending comparisons to the East Asian Tigers, which did manage to centralise their industrialisation projects under particular circumstances.

As of recent years, nonetheless, Mexico has seemingly entered yet another phase of recentralisation. As Eaton (2004) has analysed for other Latin American states throughout history, the appearance of an elected president with greater legitimacy than previous presidential figures or regimes has frequently led to recentralising dynamics. In the case of Mexico, its 2018 presidential election brought a leftist politician, Andrés Manuel López Obrador, to the presidential chair with a considerable margin of majority.

Furthermore, his party, the Movimiento de Regeneración Nacional (MORENA), in coalition with affinitive leftist parties, gained the majority of the national congress. This heightened legitimacy provided by the 2018 elections has thus created a manoeuvring capacity for the national government that had been unprecedented in Mexico since the Institutional Revolutionary Party (PRI) lost the presidential chair in 2000. Accordingly, one of the first actions announced by President López Obrador was the creation of administrative "delegates" for each of Mexico's federal entities with the role of managing social development budgets at the subnational level. This was promptly criticised by governors and political commentators alike for threatening the autonomy of subnational governments and limiting the latter's policy space.

Furthermore, the nationalist and more statist orientation that President López Obrador has regarding economic development marks the very first presidential deviation from Mexico's "neoliberal" agenda since the 1980s. Already during the first months of his presidential administration, President López Obrador has expressed a nationalist approach to industrialisation. During the month of February 2019, while presenting a new social programme in the Mexican state of Veracruz, President López Obrador clarified this nationalist turn to the country's economy by declaring, "We do want free trade and we will respect existing international agreements, but we will defend the national producer. First Mexico and then the foreign (economies)" (IDIC, 2019, p. 1).

This contrast has been quite evident in Mexico's recently liberalised oil sector. Whereas the prior presidential administration had managed to achieve a constitutional energy reform which opened the oil and electric sector to the participation of private companies, President López Obrador has already presented his National Plan for the Production of Hydrocarbons, which is based largely on the construction of another refinery plant and the rehabilitation of six existing refinery plants to fulfil Mexico's self-sufficiency in the sector with the state-owned Petróleos Mexicanos (PEMEX) at the helm. Putting the oil sector once again at the centre of the country's energy agenda, moreover, strays away from the incipient energy transition that the previous administration had begun since its adhesion to the Paris Agreement in 2015 and its formulation of "nationally determined commitments" – which had already given way to an up-and-coming "green energy" sector in Mexico.

Conclusion

As depicted in the developmental literature and economic development history, successful industrialisers were reliant on state-capital alliances, although state autonomy or authority was also essential to mobilise the entire nation and move it towards economic growth (Evans, 1995; Kohli, 2004; Weiss & Hobson, 1995). However, achieving State autonomy and an embracing centralisation has represented an ongoing challenge for large developing countries such as India, Brazil, China and Mexico. Any possibilities of achieving this centralisation have been further challenged after the multilevel conjuncture that several of these States have faced.

In the particular case of Mexico, the state's attempts to attain political control through varying pacts and arrangements with either different state levels or social groups also led to a fragmentation of its economic development drive. This lack of authority eventually perpetrated a dependence on state-capital relations which, in turn, determined economic development according to economic elites' interests. Consequently, Mexico's economic development transformed into an "arena of accommodation", as coined by Migdal (1988, p. 264) in the wider literature on the Third World states' related failures.

This fragmentation of the state's capabilities vis-à-vis economic elites seems to offer an explanatory element for understanding Mexico's ongoing incapacity to consolidate an effective economic development centre. At the turn of the new century, it was the international financial institutions and the growing presence of transnational companies (TNCs) which also constrained the federal state's autonomy regarding economic development. This leads us, in turn, to the necessity of examining Mexico's industrialisation beyond the centre in an effort to understand how effective industrial transformations did manage to crystallise. Through this perspective, the state's fragmented capacities for economic development are an illustrative factor in Mexico's current subnational variation. Furthermore, as will be argued in the case studies below, the limited capacities of the state's centre led not only to subnational variation, but to subnational determination as well.

In regards to the new presidential administration of López Obrador, his emphasis on reigniting PEMEX's refining capacities, and the budgetary resources that that demands, has once again posited the familiar "Dutch disease" as a potential threat for the country's near future. As chapter 4 will highlight, it was precisely the first-ever decentralisation of oil-related revenues that played an important role in financing Nuevo León's industrial policies. In consequence, the recentralisation of resources and the priority of reviving the oil sector as an overarching development plan could shrink the "policy space" that some subnational governments had been exploring throughout the previous decades.

References

Amsden, A. (1992). *Asia's next giant: South Korea and late industrialization.* Oxford: Oxford University Press.

Bennett, D., & Sharpe, K. (1982). The state as banker and entrepreneur: The last resort character of the Mexican State's economic intervention, 1917–1970. In *Brazil and Mexico. Patterns in late development* (pp. 165–189). Philadelphia, PA: ISHI.

Brenner, N. (2004). *New state spaces: Urban governance and the rescaling of statehood.* Oxford: Oxford University Press.

Bresser-Pereira, L. C. (2017). Two forms of capitalism: Developmentalism and economic liberalism. *Brazilian Journal of Political Economy, 37*(4), 680–703.

Dillinger, W., Perry, G., & Webb, S. B. (1999). *Macroeconomic management in decentralized democracies: The quest for hard budget constraint in Latin America.* Washington, DC: World Bank.

Doner, R. F., Ritchie, B. K., & Slater, D. (2005). Systemic vulnerability and the origins of developmental states: Northeast and Southeast Asia in comparative perspective. *International Organization, 59*(2), 327–361.

Eaton, K. (2004). *Politics beyond the capital: The design of subnational institutions in South America.* Stanford, CA: Stanford University Press.

Eaton, K. (2017). *Territory and ideology in Latin America: Policy conflicts between national and subnational governments.* Oxford: Oxford University Press.

Evans, P. (1995). *Embedded autonomy: States and industrial transformation/ Embedded autonomy.* Princeton, NJ: Princeton University Press.

Gauss, S. M. (2010). *Made in Mexico: Regions, nation, and the state in the rise of Mexican Industrialism, 1920s–1940s.* University Park, PA: Penn State University Press.

Gibson, E. (2005). Boundary control: Subnational authoritarianism in democratic countries. *World Politics, 58*(1): 101–132. Retrieved from www.jstor.org/stable/40060126

Hiskey, J. T. (2005). The political economy of subnational economic recovery in Mexico. *Latin American Research Review, 40*(1), 30–55.

Instituto Mexicano para la Competitividad (IMCO) (2015). *Reporte Deuda Subnacional.* [Online]. Retrieved February 11, 2019, from https://imco.org.mx/wp-content/uploads/2015/07/2015_Reporte_Deuda_subnacional.pdf

Instituto Mexicano para la Competitividad (IMCO) (2016). *Reporte Deuda Subnacional: Finanzas públicas.* [Online]. Retrieved February 12, 2019, from https://imco.org.mx/politica_buen_gobierno/reporte-deuda-subnacional-segundo-trimestre-de-2016/

Instituto para el Desarrollo Industrial y el Crecimiento Económico (IDIC) (2019). El momento de la verdad para la industria mexicana; Reindustrialización: el reto de la 4T. *La Voz de la Industria, 7*(141).

Jessop, B. (2015). *The state: Past, present, future.* London: John Wiley & Sons.

Johnson, C. (1982). *MITI and the Japanese miracle: The growth of industrial policy: 1925–1975.* Stanford, CA: Stanford University Press.

Hausmann, R., Rodrik, D., & Sabel, C. (2008). *Reconfiguring industrial policy: A framework with an application to South Africa.* Working paper. Cambridge, MA: John F. Kennedy School of Government.

Hooghe, L., & Marks, G. (2001). Types of multi-level governance. *European Integration Online Papers*, *5*(11).

Kohli, A. (2004). *State-directed development: Political power and industrialization in the global periphery*. Cambridge: Cambridge University Press.

May, P., & Jochim, A. (2013). Policy regime perspectives: Policies, politics, and governing. *Policy Studies Journal*, *41*(3): 426–452. doi:dx.doi.org/10.1111/psj.12024

Migdal, J. S. (1988). *Strong societies and weak states: State-society relations and state capabilities in the Third World*. Princeton, NJ: Princeton University Press.

Migdal, J. S. (2001). *State in society: Studying how states and societies transform and constitute one another*. Cambridge: Cambridge University Press.

Montero, A. P. (2002). *Shifting states in global markets: Subnational industrial policy in contemporary Brazil and Spain*. University Park, PA: Penn State University Press.

Moreno-Brid, J., & Ros, J. (2009). *Development and growth in the Mexican economy: A historical perspective*. New York, NY: Oxford University Press.

Sætren, H. (2016). From controversial policy idea to successful program implementation: the role of the policy entrepreneur, manipulation strategy, program design, institutions and open policy windows in relocating Norwegian central agencies. *Policy Sciences*, *49*(1), 71–88.

Schneider, B. R. (1999). The Desarrollista state in Brazil and Mexico. In M. Woo-Cummings (Ed.), *The developmental state* (pp. 276–305). Ithaca, NY: Cornell University Press.

Schneider, B. (2015). Designing Industrial Policy in Latin America: Business-State Relations and the New Developmentalism. New York, NY: Palgrave Macmillan.

Shils, E. (1975). *Center and periphery*. Chicago, IL: University of Chicago Press.

Sinha, A. (2003). Rethinking the developmental state model: Divided leviathan and subnational comparisons in India. *Comparative Politics*, 459–476.

Sinha, A. (2005). *The regional roots of developmental politics in India: A divided Leviathan*. Bloomington, IN: Indiana University Press.

Snyder, R. (2001a). Scaling down: The subnational comparative method. *Studies in Comparative International Development*, *36*(1), 93–110. [Online]. Retrieved September 14, 2016, from http://link.springer.com/10.1007/BF02687586

Snyder, R. (2001b). *Politics after neoliberalism: Reregulation in Mexico*. Cambridge: Cambridge University Press.

Tilly, C. (1975). *The formation of national states in Western Europe*. Princeton, NJ: Princeton University Press.

Wade, R. (1990). *Governing the market: Economic theory and the role of government in East Asian industrialization*. Princeton, NJ: Princeton University Press.

Weiss, L., & Hobson, J. M. (1995). *States and economic development: A comparative historical analysis*. London: Polity Press.

Wilson, R. H., Ward, P. M., Spink, P. K., & Rodríguez, V. E. (2008). *Governance in the Americas: Decentralization, democracy, and subnational government in Brazil, Mexico, and the USA*. Notre Dame: University of Notre Dame Press.

Yang, J. (2018). Subnational institutions and location choice of emerging market firms. *Journal of International Management*, *24*(4), 317–332.

3 Integrating subnational strategies before Mexico's trade liberalisation

Introduction

In 1962, Alexander Gerschenkron published a compilation of essays titled *Economic Backwardness in Historical Perspective*, which eventually became an analytical backbone for the developmental literature that was yet to be born with authors such as Chalmers Johnson, Peter Evans and Ha Joon-Chang. In this seminal work, Gerschenkron advanced the comparative approach of industrialisation first set out by Friedrich List's national systems of political economy. Through these essays on European industrialisation, with England seen as the role model for subsequent industrialised countries, the Russian thinker emphasised the necessity of avoiding overly generalised patterns of development in favour of trajectories in which the particular deviations of each country ended up playing a fundamental part. Or as Gerschenkron (1962, p. 44) put it: "So viewed, the industrial history of Europe appears not as a series of mere repetitions of the 'first' industrialization but as an orderly system of graduated deviations from that industrialization".

From here on out, the Russian economist pinpointed the State's role in economic development at the gravitational centre of all of his country cases. Gerschenkron also contradicted the recurring tendencies of laissez-faire or economic liberalism. In this regard, he stated that "a stronger medicine is needed than the promise of better allocation of resources or even the lower price of bread" in order to overcome a country's economic and industrial stagnation (Gerschenkron, 1962, p. 24).

One of these particularities which triggered further comparisons was precisely what Gerschenkron named "economic backwardness", a relative and, thus, comparative term for underdeveloped countries in relation to other more advanced countries. Around the same time that Gerschenkron's essays on economic backwardness were published, the Mexican state of Querétaro was trying to integrate itself into Mexico's national project of development, though with considerable structural constraints that very much represented the Russian thinker's conception of "economic backwardness": absence of pre-industrial capital, rural outlook, lack of skilled workers and, most important, a gravely deficient infrastructure not only for industrial considerations, but for the overall needs of the state's households. So could the Gerschenkronian postulates of "catching-up States" be extrapolated to subnational governments as well? And what are the factors that could facilitate or spur this industrial catching-up by Querétaro?

It might be redundant to note that subnational governments are far from being independent or completely autonomous States. At the same time, nonetheless, there are cases of subnational states, provinces or entities which have historically assembled sufficient State elements to challenge not only policy regimes from above, be it a federal or a unitary government, but also their continuation within the nation-State, as might be seen with the recent Catalonian referendum or the Calexit initiatives in California. Distinctive elements such as population, territory, culture, ideology and even statehood have increasingly encouraged separatist movements from below. The recent multilevel conjuncture has thus intensified this diffusion of attributions through different State levels, empowering subnational governments in the meantime.

This growing trend of subnational empowerment has likewise generated a distinctive approach to economic development within a globalised context. Furthermore, in the developing world, the growing empowerment of subnational governments has led to a reconsideration of the periphery feedback that subnational units had in the previous decades and are currently having (see Sinha, 2003; Montero, 2002; Gauss, 2010). So, how could we assess the more proactive and statist initiatives that have been shaped from below in the developing world? As the previous chapter highlighted in regards to the developmental State, this governmental complex generally enlisted the following elements: a nationalised emphasis on industrialisation; state leadership in development projects; a "Weberian" bureaucracy; and an emphasis on public-private collaboration despite the existence of authoritarian governments.

More recently, developmental States have been characterised as "organizational complexes in which expert and coherent bureaucratic agencies collaborate with organized private sectors to spur national growth" amid "conditions of extreme geopolitical insecurity and severe resource constraints" (Doner, Ritchie, & Slater, 2005, p. 327). According to the cited authors, the Cold War context of geopolitical frictions and the scarcity of natural resources led the East Asian Tigers to devise rather innovative and exacting development policies across their national territories to overcome their respective vulnerabilities.

In the case of Latin America, likewise, the structural deficiencies of the region's economies and the historical contingency of World War II, following a decade of economic recession, led States to formulate their own efforts in hopes of overcoming conditions of vulnerability, though with particular shortfalls in their institutional capabilities (see Bresser-Pereira, 1973; Hirschman, 1975; Schneider, 1999). One of the more relevant institutional shortfalls frequently emphasised for Latin America is the obstacle of centralisation. As has been highlighted by authors such as Huber (2003) and Gauss (2010), the shortcomings of centralisation efforts in Latin America have posed surmountable challenges for the development of the region, generating, moreover, a rather uneven landscape below the State's centre.

In the case of Mexico, as this chapter will expand through the analysis of Querétaro, the particular incapability of centralising both political and economic development led subnational governments to uneven opportunities and challenges. Therefore, just as in the case of the East Asian Tigers, Querétaro went through structural conditions of insecurity and scarcity of resources which, in turn, led its subnational government to embrace a proactive role in their industrialisation, emphasising public-private cooperation and the consolidation of their bureaucratic capabilities through institutionalised platforms. In a further echoing note, Querétaro's government fomented a public-private alliance with one of the state's bigger business groups (Ingenieros Civiles Asociados, or ICA) in resemblance to Japan's *keiretsu* and South Korea's *chaebol* involvement.

Considering subnational constraints on policymaking autonomy, however, this first case study will begin to emphasise the assessment of these industrialisation strategies more through the tenor of developmental *policy regimes* rather than developmental *States*. Throughout this book I will thus work with Eaton's (2017) re-formulation of the policy regime in the economic development realm as the "package of public policies and institutional practices that put together reflect a common set of ideas and beliefs about the appropriate role for market forces and the appropriate levels and types of state intervention" (p. 6).

The appraisal of the developmental policy regimes that have been crystallising in Mexico will raise issues of agency, structure and institutions that have been at the centre of the literature of institutional change (Mahoney & Thelen, 2009). This emphasis on the literature of institutional change will thus support a backdrop for this empirical chapter by highlighting how structural constraints or circumstances of "systemic vulnerability" (Doner et al., 2005) led governors to act as agents of policy transformation through state-society mechanisms which were gradually institutionalised at the subnational level.

Along the theoretical lines of previous sections, the present chapter will argue that the state-society collaboration arrangements that enabled Querétaro's successful catch-up were formulated at the subnational, not the national, level. Given Mexico's regionalisation and the pervasiveness of cronyism at its centre, the state-society alliances essential for developmental drives *had* to be built at a subnational level. Therefore, the present chapter will examine how subnational industrialisation strategies seem to be enlightening factors previously missing in the study of Mexico's developmentalism.

The present account, therefore, will seek to trace Querétaro's industrialisation and the actual State actors involved in it. Accordingly, this chapter will review the industrial drive that was constructed between Mexico's president, its ministries (mainly the Ministry of Hydraulic Resources, Ministry of Industry and Commerce and Ministry of Economy's General Direction of Electricity) and the governors of Querétaro. In contrast to the more centralised accounts of Mexico's *desarrollismo*, it will be particularly insightful to evidence the protagonist role that Querétaro's governors played in shaping their state's developmental policy regime and in building progressive state-society synergies into a notable approximation of an embedded autonomy, though with *desarrollista* characteristics (e.g. lack of meritocratic features).

I supported my research on Querétaro's first industrial transformation with both primary and secondary sources. The main primary sources were provided by Querétaro's Archivo Estatal, which facilitated my access to the historical documents needed to have a better perspective on Querétaro's context before and during its industrial transformation. These historical documents were governmental decrees, legislation and other historical testimonies of Querétaro at that time, such as its newspaper, *La Sombra de Arteaga*. In regards to the secondary sources used, works by Eduardo Miranda (*Del Querétaro rural al Querétaro industrial*), Digna Neri (*Industrialización y transformaciones urbanas de Querétaro: Cambios y continuidades en la Colonia Obrera, 1943–1979*) and Gustavo Ávila (*Historia socioeconómica de Querétaro*) contributed in giving the historical circumstances that were present during Querétaro's industrial transformation and the main actors that participated in this process.

The next section will first present an overview of the fragmented characteristics that Mexico has nurtured throughout its recent history with a particular emphasis on the impacts that this had on Querétaro's development. After this introduction of Querétaro in a context of backwardness, the chapter will then expand on the two independent variables that brought about Querétaro's first industrial transformation: firstly, a vertical integration with the national government and its developmental priorities, and secondly, a horizontal institutionalisation of Querétaro's industrialisation with an emphasis on public-private collaboration.

Uneven development and backward states in Mexico

As this book has argued in the preceding chapters, the particular fragmentation and unevenness of developing countries' economic and political development generated a rather galvanised configuration below the State's centre. In the case of Mexico, its colonial legacy and conflictual evolution since its independence had put the central state of Querétaro in a precarious position. The present chapter's puzzle is consequently in line with the traditional developmental puzzle, although at a subnational level. How did Querétaro, a marginalised and poor state entering the 1950s, manage to catch up with the industrial capacities of the more industrialised states, such as Nuevo León, Jalisco and Puebla?

Overall, Querétaro very well sums up what a "backward state" looked like during the first half of the 20th century in Mexico. It is a state from the central-west region – a region named the Bajío. It is the 27th smallest state in Mexico out of 32 states, and during the 1940s and 1950s, Querétaro was hallmarked by economic stagnation, along with alarming rates of poverty and marginalisation in a highly rural context. Around the same time, Querétaro's central water-sewage infrastructure still relied on a sewage canal dating all the way back to colonial times (Neri, 2013). Its water resources were dismal and insufficient for its agrarian activities, let alone for an expansion of industry.

This rather primitive sewage system was not only an economic problem, but a health problem as well. During the first half of the 20th century, its lagging capabilities constantly generated pandemics among the population and cattle stocks (García, 2011). Querétaro's electrical capacities ran along similar lines, receiving only 8,600 kilowatts in total for all of its economic and urban activities. This meagre availability led to constant power outages, black-outs and government-imposed rationing of electricity, which sometimes lasted 24 hours. Querétaro was among many states in Mexico with insufficient electricity. Around this time, therefore, even the country's presidents acknowledged that "more than half of Mexico's population lacked access to electrical services" (Ruiz, 2006, p. 22).

At the national level, however, 1940 became a landmark year for Mexico's commitment to national industrialisation. As in other successful developmental stories, the presence of war among nations turned out to be a rather positive spur for growth. World War II came to offer, as stated by Miranda regarding Mexico's case (2005, p. 114), a "natural protection" which obliged its economy to produce its own manufactures and outputs, considering that their otherwise traditional purveyor, the United States, was occupied with its own war-time affairs.

When the war was over, however, a more active form of protectionism was put in place by President Miguel Alemán (1946–1952) using macro-economic policies. In the first year of his administration, President Alemán decreed the Law for the Development of the Manufacturing Industry, which increased incentives for manufacturing industries with tax exemptions, protective tariffs and licences, plus the elimination of import duties for heavy machinery. But how could Querétaro insert itself into this national drive towards industrialisation amid a stagnant economy and infrastructure?

With the Law for the Development of the Manufacturing Industry of President Alemán, issued in 1946, many tax exemptions on imports and fiscal-related incentives were given to establish new industries or factories. But Querétaro was not Monterrey with substantial amounts of capital and sufficient water and electrical resources. Nor was it Mexico City or its neighbouring Estado de Mexico, in which, along with Nuevo León, much of the country's capital and infrastructure were also concentrated. It is no surprise then that during the first half of the ISI period, new industries were concentrated around Nuevo León and Mexico City, with 24% of NAFINSA (Nacional Financiera, Mexico's National Development Bank) credits, for example, going to Monterrey and its surrounding cities (Septien, 2005). Afterwards, in 1955, a Law for New and Necessary Industries was created to promote the creation or improvement of manufacturing activities, but 90% of the enterprises benefitted by the fiscal incentives of this law ended up being established in Mexico City, its neighbour Estado de Mexico, and Nuevo León through the 1970s (ECLAC, 1979).

A large part of this concentration was enhanced by Mexico's regulatory capture via the Finance Ministry. Through this capture, the Finance Ministry began formulating Mexico's economic development by catering to the big business groups formed around Monterrey (capital city of Nuevo León), Guadalajara, Mexico City and Estado de Mexico (Maxfield, 1990). Infrastructure, the main constraint on the country's development, was negotiated directly between Mexico's central offices and these economic elites (Alemán, 2006), while public subsidies were an "all-out government support" for the same "private investors" (Erfani, 1995, pp. 89–90).

Up to this day, Mexico's economic development remains caught in a vicious circle regarding infrastructure. Economic officials (interviews, 2015) at the state level constantly decry how investments do not arrive in particular regions because of a lack of infrastructure. Also, they relate how infrastructures are not constructed by the federal government because of a lack of economic investments or productive activities in the same region; circumstances reminiscent of Hirschman's (1958, p. 36) accounts of "vicious circles" in industrialising efforts by underdeveloped countries.

Accordingly, during Mexico's ISI period (1940–1982), public investment became the "most dynamic factor of economic growth" because it was "the main instrument to create the basic infrastructure" (Miranda, 2005, p. 188). Querétaro's annual budget, however, was among the lowest of Mexico's states, and 90% of federal and subnational economic resources were controlled centrally by the federal government. The vicious circle in Querétaro seemed to go round and round following Mexico's independence: no infrastructure due to a lack of investment resources, and no investment resources (either foreign or local) due to a lack of infrastructure.

Thus, by the time Mexico started its nationwide drive towards industrialisation with its ISI initiative, Querétaro was among the more lagging and marginalised states. With a devastated economy and a substantially disabled infrastructure, Querétaro's chances of catching up with other industrialised states seemed like a fantasy. Nonetheless, as will be depicted in the following section, a twofold strategy led by subsequent governors of Querétaro began to give this Mexican state a brighter outlook: firstly, a vertical integration with the national government's actors and economic priorities, and secondly, a horizontal institutionalisation of public-private cooperation directed towards the state's industrial transformation.

Vertical integration: modernising Querétaro's infrastructure

Evans' (1997a) study on developing countries contains case studies which revolve around state-society synergies woven to transform the infrastructure capabilities as a stepping stone for further development. In it, Fung's (1997) case study examines how reiterative cooperation and interaction between local farmers and local officials enhanced the capacities of Taiwan's irrigation system. Likewise, in the study of Ostrom (1997), synergistic interactions between state and society are visible and essential tools in upgrading Brazil's water and sanitation works. In a more systemic analysis of subnational strategies towards growth, however, there is generally an obstacle which impedes industrial take-off or industrial transformation: the lack of resources. In Latin America, in either unitary or federal governments, the insufficiency of fiscal and financial resources has generally been at the heart of the region's political, let alone economic, development (see Eaton, 2004). Sometimes the capacity to access these economic resources held by the national government is the toughest task for subnational governments looking to promote their state's industrialisation.

In Querétaro, following the developmental drive of the national government since the 1940s, subsequent governors formulated several laws and public policies to promote the state's industrialisation (Congreso del Estado de Querétaro, 1944). Due to the lack of electrical infrastructure, however, local factories and enterprises began falling into bankruptcy. Therefore, this lack of infrastructure quickly became the central concern of both society and government in Querétaro, but neither had sufficient economic resources to cover the cost. In 1949, for instance, Querétaro's annual budget amounted to just 1.6 million pesos, "the most meagre and exiguous" budget of all the Mexican states (Miranda, 2005, p. 162).

Querétaro was among many states in Mexico with insufficient electricity. The electrical industry had not yet been nationalised, but the state-owned enterprise Comisión Federal de Electricidad (CFE; Federal Commission of Electricity) was already consolidating as the government's agent in providing, regulating and incentivising Mexico's electrification programme. Along with CFE, two other enterprises – which were foreign-owned – "practically held control of the industry": the American and Foreign Power Light and the Mexican Light and Power Company (López, 2006a, p. 83). Thus, in the words of President Ruiz Cortines (2006, p. 22), "government, as a way to strengthen the Federal Commission of Electricity, gave an equitable treatment to private enterprises, so that without trumping any consumer interests, it might be an incentive for them to expand and upgrade their installations".

But this "equitable" treatment basically represented a 50/50 investment participation in joint programmes of electrification – investments which were far beyond the local capacities of Querétaro. Since the preceding administration of President Miguel Alemán, when public investment in infrastructure gradually became the piston for economic development, projects were generally negotiated between the federal government and the industrialists involved, with a fair share of cronyism. The federal Ministry of Economy held negotiations directly with industrialists, "who required consumption levels above 400 kilowatts, with the objective of providing them with the facilities for them to acquire their own power plants of electrical fluid" (Alemán, 2006, p. 21).

But small industrialists from Querétaro did not have the necessary capital to acquire their own plants, or provide half of the investments required for these infrastructural projects. To further aggravate matters, the foreign-owned electrical Compañía Hidroeléctrica de Querétaro, which seemed like the only enterprise capable of upgrading the state's infrastructure, constantly proved to be a difficult partner to both the federal and subnational state. This company insisted that its participation and investment be conditioned by substantial increases to electrical tariffs, in what later was characterised by the President as "greedy petitions" (Miranda, 2005, p. 220).

The Government of Querétaro was then left almost by itself. Their resources were well under the required minimum, considering that the federal government had already taken command of 90% of the nation's fiscal resources (Meyer, 1981). Consequently, there was little chance for Querétaro to upgrade its infrastructure capacities, with either public or private resources; hence, the vicious cycle of lack of infrastructure due to lack of investment, and lack of investment due to lack of infrastructure.

Nonetheless, both state and society in Querétaro began to acknowledge that Mexico's presidents and its federal ministries held the keys to tending to Querétaro's infrastructural needs. With this in mind, they organised themselves to try to land federal programmes of infrastructure in Querétaro. On society's part, the actors were plenty: the Chamber of National Commerce of Querétaro, the Chamber of National Commerce on a Small Scale of Querétaro, the National Chamber of the Transformative Industry in Querétaro, the Patronal Centre of Querétaro, the Federation of Workers from Querétaro, the Local Agricultural Association of the Centre, the Local Cattle Breeders Association of the Centre, El Hércules Textiles and La Queretana Textiles. Representing Querétaro's entrepreneurial society, they signed a petition and sent it to President Alemán, stating the "grave damages and constraints" that were being inflicted on Querétaro's economy due to the absence of electrical capacities (Miranda, 2005, p. 205).

Meanwhile, Governor Pozito, in turn, wrote frequently to the Ministry of Economy regarding the pertinence of infrastructural developments in his state. Finally, President Alemán gave in. He agreed to expand Querétaro's hydro-electrical capacities, although on one condition: that Querétaro's government and/or private investors contribute 50% of the costs, which were around 3 million pesos in total. With a meagre subnational budget almost surpassed by the required investment, the electrification project was eventually dismissed.

As a response to this unattended predicament, Querétaro society mobilised until the Comité ProDefensa Social de Querétaro (Committee for the Social Defence of Querétaro) was established in February 1955. It was created by the same groups who had earlier sent a letter to the preceding president on the same matter: chambers of commerce and industry, commercial and non-commercial associations, workers' unions and lawyers, among other small-scale economic actors. Its first action as a committee was to send a telegram to President Ruiz Cortines and, a month later, a letter restating the dire conditions of Querétaro's electricity resources.

This committee, furthermore, was also active in framing the lack of electrical capacities as one of the central problems of its state. It constantly lobbied the president, the Ministry of Economy and CFE; it conducted technical studies, created proposals for new electrical plants and suggested that

CFE acquire the foreign-owned Compañía Hidroeléctrica de Querétaro, as this company had already become an obstacle to negotiating electrical projects between the state and the private sector.

After several back and forth communications and studies, the federal government and CFE's solution was to connect Querétaro with a new electrical plant, El Cóbano. This connection was relatively successful: it fulfilled Querétaro's needs at the time, up to 75%, substantially diminishing the rationalisation measures and power shortages (Ruiz, 2006). But the needs of the time or, rather, 75% of the needs, were well below the electrical resources necessary for more integral industrialisation.

Consequently, as these electrical capabilities were still pending, the Comité ProDefensa, along with Governor Mondragón, sent the federal government a technical study that proposed to connect Querétaro to the electrical plants that provided Mexico City with electricity. Nevertheless, the electrical plant feeding Mexico City was owned by one of the electrical industry's giants: the Mexican Light and Power Company.

By the first decades of the 20th century, the Mexican Light and Power Company, founded during the Porfirian regime and financed by Canadian capital, was the electrical TNC with the most economic power in Mexico's electrical sector. Just as its economic power had grown during the first decades of the past century, so too had "its resistance" against the state's initiative or the "necessity to regulate and have a better control of its national resources" (Terán, 2015, p. 115). By 1937, it provided Mexico City, Puebla, Hidalgo, Estado de Mexico and Michoacán with electricity and controlled 50% of the electrical resources in the country (ibid.).

At first, given Querétaro's still rural outlook, the Canadian enterprise proved rather reluctant to provide these services as the return investment seemed rather shaky. Joint negotiations consequently ensued between these different actors: the Comité ProDefensa, Querétaro's Governor, the federal government through its General Direction of Electricity and the Canadian TNC. Finally, after these intermeshed negotiations in which both the federal and state governments had to accept Mexican Light and Power's conditions of raising electrical tariffs in Querétaro, the state was finally provided with an additional 25,000 kilowatts through connection to the Michoacán plant. With this, Querétaro finally had sufficient electricity for potential industrialisation.

After this electrification project, Querétaro's industrial future seemed ever more promising. According to the historian Eduardo Miranda (2005), "in 1956, with the energy transmitted both by the El Cóbano plant and the Tuxtepec line, the state of Querétaro, especially its capital city, was in better conditions to respond to the demand of (electrical) supply of enterprises of complex manufacturing that looked to establish in there" (pp. 215–216).

Some years later, in 1960, the constant frictions in negotiations between foreign-owned enterprises and the Mexican State eventually led President López Mateos to nationalise the electrical industry, as it was already central to the federal government's agenda. In the president's expressed views, this action meant the "culmination of a vindication process, inspired in the purest patriotism" (López, 2006a, p. 85).

Shortly afterwards, in 1969, a national system of electricity was consolidated with Querétaro as one of its corollaries within the Centre and Bajío region. The General Director of CFE mentioned this step of providing Querétaro with its own electrical sub-station as a fundamental tool for Mexico's industrial decentralisation and a clear sign of support from the President for Querétaro with its traditions of "work, social peace and growth of industrial wealth" (Miranda, 2005, p. 224). Thus, in less than three decades, Querétaro had worked against all the odds until it had positioned itself in the centre of Mexico's electrical distribution system.

Horizontal institutionalisation in Querétaro's first industrial transformation

Throughout the 1950s, growth was slow as it was still highly constrained by Querétaro's lagging infrastructure. During the first half of this decade, Kellogg's was the only large-scale enterprise established within this state. It was not until 1958, with the construction of the Querétaro-México highway and the electrical plant of El Cóbano, that some bigger factories turned their eyes to Querétaro. In this year, TNCs such as Ralston Purina (agro-industrial) and Singer (electro-domestic) were established in Querétaro's de facto industrial zone – Hacienda La Era.

With the upgrade of its infrastructure, Querétaro finally began to be seen as having potential within the world of Mexico's industrialisation (see González & Osorio, 2000). The resounding industrial take-off of Querétaro thus took place in the 1960s, when a more thorough state-business alliance was built between the Governor, Francisco González de Cosío (1961–1967), and Bernardo Quintana, Director of Grupo ICA – a leading group of industrialists in engineering and construction activities from Mexico's capital. Finally, through this public-private allegiance, Governor González was able to scale up the state's industrial activities into Mexico's national ISI drive. In this sense, he consolidated the role of Querétaro's governor as a "binding agent" of industrialisation: an actor who sets the optimal path for growth whilst eliciting the necessary state-society coalitions (see Hirschman, 1958).

Accordingly, the principal joint project between the governor and the engineer Quintana was about building a more attractive industrial zone in Querétaro to trigger its industrialisation. After negotiating favourable prices and tax exemptions with the governor, Grupo ICA acquired over 8.26 million square metres of industrial estate property in order to refurbish it and transform it into what became Querétaro's emblematic Parques Industriales (industrial estates). These industrial estates, also named "Satellite City", "were financed by the same group (Grupo ICA)" and included every urban service, gas infrastructure, a residential area for employers and employees and even a commercial plaza (Arvizu, 2005, p. 223).

Querétaro's government, in turn, expropriated large estates to build a public industrial zone with the corresponding approval from the President – as was demanded by federal laws and regulations governing expropriation matters. Then, instead of competing with offers of industrial estates to national and foreign investors, Grupo ICA and Querétaro's government worked as a pair in attracting different niches of industrialists: Industrial Parks demanded much higher prices due to top-end facilities while the public estates offered lower prices and lower-end facilities. These joint bids for landing investments were highly successful as they were supported by the industrial incentives contemplated in Querétaro's Law 93.

In the meantime, and just as important as this alliance, Governor González institutionalised Querétaro's state-society synergies within the Consejo Económico de Querétaro (Querétaro's Economic Council). As a result, a more formalised approximation of an embedded autonomy began to be consolidated. Governor González's initiative proved to be an efficient way of incorporating Querétaro's growing social forces into a joint project of transformation. In its constitutional decree, it was stated that the Council was created "as an organ of the State's Government with the objective of studying the problems inherent to agricultural and industrial production of the entity" (Congreso de Querétaro, 1961, p. 240). The Council was integrated by a president and a secretary general named directly by the governor, along with councillors who represented the "most significant sectors of the Entity's economy" (Congreso de Querétaro, 1961, p. 240).

In the first meeting of this Council, for instance, its members included two ex-governors, the Chancellor of the Autonomous University of Querétaro, a renowned industrialist of the capital, and the President of Querétaro's Chamber of Commerce, along with the state government's representatives. Among the main functions of this Council were the following: planning Querétaro's economic development, defining which industries should be incentivised and protected, defining Querétaro's infrastructure priorities and guiding private capital's cooperation towards the realisation of public works and the general services needed for Querétaro's economic development.

One of the Council's first actions was, accordingly, to map out Querétaro's industrial prospects by contracting the services of Arthur D. Little, a firm from the United States. This firm eventually mapped out Querétaro's industrial advantages (mainly its geographical location) and the three industrial sectors that could be readily nourished: processed foods, metallic products and the *maquila* industry (Arvizu, 2005). Around this time, at the national level, the second stage of ISI in Mexico began to take shape as an overarching goal of the federal government. Its aim was to develop Mexico's capacities in producing its own intermediary and capital goods. In this process, the Ministry of Industry and Commerce (MIC) was put in charge of implementing the corresponding measures. The main tools that this MIC deployed were the "previous permits" or import licences, through which the federal government supported the import of the goods and machinery needed for industrialisation and prohibited those considered to obstruct it.

Therefore, with the coordination of Querétaro's Economic Council and its enhanced sharing of information, Governor González scaled up the industrialising needs of local industrialists, or potential local industrialists, into the platform regulated by the MIC. Accordingly, Querétaro's government became the main agent or facilitator in getting the "previous permits" requested by Querétaro's industrial community, and, likewise, in acceding to public subsidies which could be targeted for the state's industrial activities (Miranda, 2005, p. 306).

It was during the existence of this Economic Council and its synergistic interactions that the industrial take-off of Querétaro crystallised. Querétaro was suddenly able to contribute to Mexico's ISI. In their Industrial Parks, in 1963, Grupo ICA established its conglomerate Industria de Hierro with an initial investment of 48.4 million pesos, which was then multiplied by federal credits from Mexico's development bank NAFINSA and the Inter-American Development Bank (Ávila, 2008). Soon after, Industria de Hierro became one of the main constructors of Mexico's infrastructure, with projects such as dams, machinery, bridges and Mexico City's airport and subway. It created substantial linkages with Querétaro's smaller industrialists and diversified its production through the creation of other related enterprises – such as Speed Belt, Huber and Fimsa, all mainly involved in the manufacturing of heavy machinery.

Two years later, Grupo ICA made an alliance with the North American consortium Clark Equipment to establish the automotive sector enterprise Transmisiones y Equipos Mecánicos (Tremec) with an initial investment of 190 million pesos. Tremec, however, was established in the government's industrial zone, rather than in the ICA's Industrial Parks, in order to support Governor González's "interest . . . in promoting the industrial zone of the State" (Miranda, 2005, pp. 379–380).

Parallel to Industria de Hierro's leadership in the construction sector, Tremec rapidly consolidated itself as a national leader in the automotive sector. Before the end of the 1960s, Tremec was the national leader in the fabrication of automotive transmissions and one of the main exporters to the United States after it managed to partner with Ford Motors as a supplier. In this sense, Tremec also became one of the principal agents of Mexico's ISI in a sector as vital as the automotive.

Governor González's agency for Querétaro's development was, nonetheless, far from over. It had to extend the same enthusiasm to TNCs which seemed to offer an industrial-upgrading opportunity for Querétaro's industry – according to the Economic Council's prioritised sectors and activities. Clear evidence of the governor's promotion of industry was portrayed in his negotiations with the MIC in order to establish the British company Massey Ferguson in Querétaro. When Governor González first gave notice to the MIC of Massey Ferguson's intention to establish in Querétaro as a promising opportunity for resolving Mexico's scarcity of tractors and agricultural machinery, the project was rejected. The arguments made by the MIC were that there were already too many competitors in the sector, stating that another enterprise in the sector, besides the established Ford and International Harvester, would oversaturate the market. In the words of Governor González, an effort at negotiating was necessary:

> I had to make an in-depth study to demonstrate that the tractors of Massey Ferguson constituted 42 percent of the machines used in Mexico's agriculture. I told them that if this brand was not produced, it would impoverish 42 percent of the users, meaning, the agriculture producers who used the brand, given that none of its replacement parts would be produced, nor a system of maintenance would be facilitated.
>
> (Miranda, 2005, pp. 391–392)

By the end of Governor González's administration, the industrial outlook of Querétaro had been cast amid the country's second stage of ISI through the participation of both foreign and Mexican capital. After the end of this administration, the new administration of Juventino Castro (1967–1973) reshaped Querétaro's Economic Council into the Committee for the Industrial Development of the State of Querétaro (CODIQUE). This committee worked in a similar way to its predecessor, though it was now headed by Grupo ICA's Director, Bernardo Quintana, who spearheaded negotiations with potential investors to settle their businesses in Querétaro.

The main advantages offered in these negotiations were the fiscal and economic incentives offered by Querétaro's Law 93, which consisted mainly of tax cuts and donations of industrial estates. Soon, the amount of industrial progress was evident. Throughout the 1960s, this included industrial investment growing by 668.2%, industrial outputs increasing by 760%, and employment increasing by 448.8%, along with a doubling of the number of industrial establishments (Miranda, 2005, p. 364).

In the meantime, these same actors were emphatic at upgrading Queré-taro's human capital, instead of importing it from leading industrial poles such as Monterrey, Guadalajara and Mexico City. They coordinated initiatives with the Autonomous University of Querétaro and created – with federal funds which were lobbied for, and public and private donations – several technical institutions, such as the Tecnológico Regional de Queré-taro, Escuela Técnica Industrial número 59 and Capacitation Centre for Industrial Labour 17 (CECATI) (Ávila, 2008).

Likewise, as these state-society synergies made efforts to upgrade Queré-taro's labour force and insert it into the nascent arena of industrialisation, they made sure to also insert local merchants and small industrialists into the productive chains of the big TNCs. This was, in fact, a key element in achieving Querétaro's social or developmental consensus. Not only were small and medium entrepreneurs receiving the same microeconomic incentives as TNCs, but Querétaro's government, its Economic Council and, later, CODIQUE were making emphatic efforts in linking them as suppliers into the TNCs' production processes.

As a minister of government of Querétaro related during the 1960s (in Miranda, 2005, p. 350), when the big factories and TNCs first arrived in Querétaro, they first asked what kind of suppliers and services could be found there. This minister, in a practice that was also paralleled by Queréta-ro's chambers of commerce and industry, promptly established the linkages between local suppliers and arriving factories. Along these lines, commerce and services also saw a substantial increase in growth rates throughout the 1960s. Investment capital in commercial activities grew fivefold, total sales fourfold, and employment in commerce and the number of commercial establishments doubled. In service activities, the growth was also evident: total income and employment grew threefold, while invested capital and the number of establishments grew to 150% (Miranda, 2005).

By the beginning of the 1970s, Querétaro had garnered a reputation as a state with advanced levels of industrialisation. Furthermore, President Echeverría's attempts at dismembering the persistent practices of cronyism dominant at the national level had a lasting impact on Querétaro. During his first year in the administration, 1970, President Echeverría was emphatic on the true possibility of making national growth and a more equal distribution of wealth compatible. This was because not only was growth being concentrated in three metropolitan areas (Mexico City and its neighbour-ing Estado de Mexico, Monterrey and Guadalajara), but its profits were also being concentrated in the hands of a few economic elites (Bennett & Sharpe, 1982, p. 169).

In a complementary response by a federal legislator to one of Echever-ría's presidential addresses, this initiative was summarised as follows (in Echeverría, 2006, p. 172): "In a word, Mexico, with its Government, has chosen the democratic path toward a shared development, not a development for the fortunate, not a development for the rich, not a development for the powerful".

Along these "shared development" lines, President Echeverría launched his decrees on industrial decentralisation (1971–1972) and his Programme for the Promotion of Industrial Estates and Commercial Centres. In this initiative, incentives for new industries and the construction of new Industrial Estates were favoured with tax incentives when established in regions outside the three metropolises of Mexico City (and Estado de México), Monterrey and Guadalajara, which in 1970 combined to make up 25% of the population and 60% of the country's manufacturing outputs (Tello, 2010).

The results of these initiatives were nonetheless ambiguous. Even though the aforementioned cities evidenced a *desaceleración* (Guadarrama & Olivera, 2001), or loss of industrial momentum, the industrial activities continued to concentrate around those pioneering nuclei of growth. In 1970, for example, the three cited metropolises had a participation of 49.4% in the country's total of industrial outputs; in 1996, that percentage dropped to 37.1%, with the difference of 12% migrating to neighbouring states (based on statistics from Guadarrama & Olivera, 2001, p. 34).

Nevertheless, with these initiatives, Querétaro clearly benefitted from the migration of industrial activities from the abovementioned cities and from the installation of the ambitious Industrial Park, Ciudad Industrial Benito Juárez. The remaining 12% of industrial activities thus migrated mainly to neighbouring states in the Bajío and Centre regions, such as Querétaro, Puebla and Aguascalientes.

Many of those industries installed themselves in Querétaro's Ciudad Industrial Benito Juárez due to Querétaro's industrial incentives – including the glass manufacturer Vitro, the agro-industrial TNC Clemente Jacques,

Table 3.1 Rates of manufacturing GDP annual growth in Mexican states from the Centre and Bajío regions (1970–1988)

	1970–1980	1980–1988	1970–1988
Centre			
Federal District	5.30%	−2.50%	1.40%
Estado de México	7.10%	0.60%	3.85%
Neighbouring states			
Querétaro	**11.30%**	**6.70%**	**9.00%**
Tlaxcala	9.10%	6.50%	7.80%
Morelos	9.00%	5.30%	7.15%

Source: Author's elaboration based on data from Guadarrama and Olivera (2001).

large textile factories such as Polinova and Celanese, and small and medium enterprises (SMEs) in the automotive sector, such as Fluval, Miscar and Tecnoman. The success of Ciudad Industrial Benito Juárez thus marked Querétaro's definite consolidation as one of Mexico's industrial leaders (INEGI, 1986). And Querétaro barely managed to do so, for the decade of the 1970s marked an irreversible slow-down, and eventual shutdown, of Mexico's state-led model of industrialisation.

Conclusion

As argued throughout the present chapter, Querétaro's industrialist catching-up was mainly driven from a subnational platform. In the process, state-society synergies and the translation of national developmental goals into a local context generated higher-impact industrial policies (including incentives, attraction of national and foreign investment, upgrading of infrastructure and lobbying efforts) which were essential for overcoming the subnational context of "economic backwardness". It is through these subnational processes that the periphery feedback and multilevel aspects of Mexico's *desarrollismo* can be better witnessed.

The uneven support of Mexico's central ministries (mainly the Finance Ministry) for a few Mexican states initially excluded Querétaro from integrating itself into the national developmentalist project, propagating the vicious circle of lack of investment and lack of infrastructure. However, it was the scarcity of resources and the generalised sense of insecurity, which resonates with East Asian Tigers' conditions of "systemic vulnerability" (Doner et al., 2005), that triggered the need for weaving a joint project of transformation between state and society.

In this sense, Querétaro's state and society coalitions had to row up-stream to gain access to the national platform of industrialisation. In these efforts of vertical integration, state-society alliances were an essential factor in Querétaro's scaling-up success – in terms of both infrastructure and industrialisation. Throughout the 1960s, the institutionalisation of these state-society synergies in Querétaro's Economic Council and, later, CODIQUE marked the epitome of a state-society joint project of transformation. Furthermore, the legal frameworks formulated by Querétaro's governors to incentivise industry, particularly Law 93, also contributed to the institutionalisation of Querétaro's industrial policy.

Through these institutions, Querétaro's governors were able to incorporate economic agents and convince them to develop what Evans called the "dual character" of business: pursuing profits and, at the same time, being a source of "productive-enhancing" investments (Evans, 1997b, p. 63). In this sense, Querétaro achieved a better approximation to an embedded autonomy or a horizontal embeddedness which, in contrast, failed to crystallise at the national level. During this process, Querétaro's governors correspondingly became the main agents of their state's industrial transformation from the 1940s until the end of the 1970s, embracing the challenging task of integrating their state's interests into the national agenda. And although the state's governors changed every six years, the fact that they all were from the PRI allowed them to pursue a continuous and cohesive framework of industrial policies.

Given Mexico's inefficient and partially captured *desarrollista* centre, Querétaro's case is rather useful in illuminating the multilevel aspect of its catching-up. In other words, the present chapter seems a more rewarding attempt at linking micro- to macro-level change by showing where the actual transformations of the State were happening (see Migdal, 2001). It is worth noting that this radical transformation of Querétaro, from being a backward rural state to an industrialised state, was supported through an interscalar compatibility of developmental or *desarrollista* policy regimes.

Both the federal and subnational governments were configuring public policies to trigger economic development through industrial means. Despite the pervasive cronyism at the federal level, this *desarrollista* drive was supported by protectionism, national industrialisation and high rates of investment in infrastructure – all of which were exploited by Querétaro's subnational governments in a timely manner in order to overcome their context of economic backwardness.

A multileveled approximation to Mexico's industrialisation, such as the one explored throughout this chapter, provides a better testimony to which of the State's actors or ministries were more involved in the process and what role they were playing. During Querétaro's industrial transformation, Mexico's federal ministries (i.e. the Finance Ministry and MIC) played either a financing or a regulatory role in Mexico's ISI. In contrast, Querétaro's governors played the more integral role of binding agents for their state's industrial transformation.

As a result, these governors had a leading role in attracting investment, fostering new industries and, also, setting up adequate infrastructure and cooperative mechanisms to consolidate Querétaro's industrialisation. In the meantime, subsequent governors of Querétaro, Governor González in particular, managed to adapt the national drive towards industrialisation into a locally transformed policy regime that underlined the priorities of integrating local enterprises, landing productive investments and upgrading workers' skills. Overall, the continuity of a cohesive set of industrial policies shaped a developmental policy regime which contributed in scaling Querétaro's industrialisation efforts onto national and international platforms.

References

Alemán, M. (2006). *Informes presidenciales de Alemán Valdés*. Mexico: Congreso de la Unión.

Arvizu, C. (2005). *Evolución urbana de Querétaro*. Querétaro: Tecnológico de Monterrey.

Ávila, G. (2008). *Historia socioeconómica de Querétaro*. Mexico: Secretaría de Educación Pública.

Bennett, D., & Sharpe, K. (1982). The state as banker and entrepreneur: The last resort character of the Mexican State's economic intervention, 1917–1970. In *Brazil and Mexico. Patterns in Late Development* (pp. 165–189). Philadelphia, PA: ISHI.

Bresser-Pereira, L. C. (1973). O novo modelo brasileiro de desenvolvimento, *Revista Dados, 11*, 122–145.

Congreso del Estado de Querétaro (1944*). Ley número 33*, Querétaro: Congreso del Estado de Querétaro.

Congreso del Estado de Querétaro (1961). *La Sombra de Arteaga*, Querétaro: Congreso del Estado de Querétaro.

Doner, R. F., Ritchie, B. K., & Slater, D. (2005). Systemic vulnerability and the origins of developmental states: Northeast and Southeast Asia in comparative perspective. *International Organization, 59*(2), 327–361.

Eaton, K. (2004). *Politics beyond the capital: The design of subnational institutions in South America*. Stanford, CA: Stanford University Press.

Eaton, K. (2017). *Territory and ideology in Latin America: Policy conflicts between national and subnational governments*. Oxford: Oxford University Press.

Echeverría, L. (2006). *Informes presidenciales de Echeverría Álvarez*. Mexico: Congreso de la Unión.

Economic Commission for Latin America and the Caribbean (ECLAC) (1979). *Principales rasgos del proceso de industrialización y de la política industrial de México en la década de los setenta*. Mexico: ECLAC.

Erfani, J. A. (1995). *The paradox of the Mexican state: Rereading sovereignty from independence to NAFTA*. Boulder, CO: Riener.

Evans, P. (1997a). *State-society synergy: Government and social capital in development*. Berkeley: University of California at Berkeley.

Evans, P. (1997b). State structures, government business relations, and economic transformation. In *Business and the state in developing countries* (pp. 63–87). Ithaca: Cornell University Press.

Fung, W. (1997). Institutional design of public agencies and coproduction: A study of irrigation associations in Taiwan. In *State-society synergy: Government and social capital in development*. Berkeley: University of California at Berkeley.

García, M. (2011). *Querétaro. Historia breve*. Mexico: Fondo de Cultura Económica.

Gauss, S. M. (2010). *Made in Mexico: Regions, nation, and the state in the rise of Mexican industrialism, 1920s–1940s*. University Park, PA: Penn State University Press.

Gerschenkron, A. (1962). *Economic backwardness in historical perspective*. Cambridge, MA: Belknap Press of Harvard University Press.

González, C. I., & Osorio, L. E. (2000). *Cien años de industria en Querétaro.* Querétaro: Universidad Autónoma de Querétaro.

Guadarrama, J., & Olivera, G. (2001). Desaceleración, crisis, reactivación y recesión industrial de la región Centro de México. Un largo ciclo de reestructuración del núcleo y la periferia. *EURE* (pp. 65–100).

Hirschman, A. O. (1958). *The strategy of economic development.* New Haven, CT: Yale University Press.

Hirschman, A. O. (1975). Policymaking and policy analysis in Latin America—a return journey. *Policy Sciences, 6*(4), 385–402.

Huber, E. (2003). *Models of capitalism: Lessons for Latin America.* University Park, PA: Penn State University Press.

Instituto Nacional de Estadística y Geografía (INEGI) (1986). *Estructura económica del estado de Querétaro.* Mexico: Instituto Nacional de Estadística y Geografía.

López, A. (2006a). *Informes presidenciales de López Mateos.* Mexico: Congreso de la Unión.

López, J. (2006b). *Informes presidenciales de López Portillo.* México: Congreso de la Unión.

Mahoney, J., & Thelen, K. (Eds.). (2009). *Explaining institutional change: ambiguity, agency, and power.* Cambridge: Cambridge University Press.

Maxfield, S. (1990). *Governing capital: International finance and Mexican politics.* Ithaca: Cornell University Press.

Meyer, L. (1981). La Encrucijada. In *Historia general de México.* México: El Colegio de México.

Migdal, J. S. (2001). *State in society: Studying how states and societies transform and constitute one another.* Cambridge: Cambridge University Press.

Miranda, E. (2005). *Del Querétaro rural al Querétaro industrial: 1940–1973.* Mexico: Editorial Porrúa.

Montero, A. P. (2002). *Shifting states in global markets: Subnational industrial policy in contemporary Brazil and Spain.* University Park, PA: Penn State University Press.

Neri, D. (2013). *Industrialización y transformaciones urbanas de Querétaro. Cambios y continuidades en la Colonia Obrera, 1943–1979.* Querétaro: Universidad Autónoma de Querétaro.

Ostrom, E. (1997). Crossing the great divide: Coproduction, synergy, and development. In *State-society synergy: Government and social capital in development.* Berkeley: University of California at Berkeley.

Ruiz, A. (2006). *Informes Presidencial de Adolfo Ruiz Cortines.* México: Congreso de la Unión.

Schneider, B. R. (1999). The Desarrollista state in Brazil and Mexico. In M. Woo-Cummings (Ed.), *The developmental state* (pp. 276–305). Ithaca, NY: Cornell University Press.

Septién, M. (2005). *Historia de Querétaro.* Querétaro: Asociación de Libreros de Querétaro.

Sinha, A. (2003). Rethinking the developmental state model: Divided leviathan and subnational comparisons in India. *Comparative Politics*, 459–476.

Tello, C. (2010). *Sobre la desigualdad en México*. Mexico: Universidad Nacional Autónoma de México.

Terán, A. (2015). Análisis histórico de la nacionalización de la Comisión Federal de Electricidad y sus implicaciones políticas y económicas para México. *Jornadas de Historia Económica del Colegio de México*.

4 Subnational strategies after Mexico's trade liberalisation

Nuevo León

Introduction

During the 1980s, the PRI government put an end to Mexico's ISI model which had prevailed over the previous four decades, undertaking instead a radical neoliberal shift following the International Monetary Fund's structural adjustment packages (SAPs). It was *fracasomanía* all over again. And the radical adoption of neoliberal policies was eventually associated with Mexico's "lost decade" of the 1980s (Panizza, 2009; Whitehead, 2006). The State's retreat from promoting economic development was felt across the economy. From 1935 to 1982, public investment had grown at an annual rate of over 8%; from 1983 to the start of the new century, in contrast, it was reduced to a mere 2% (Calva, 2010). This led ultimately to a greater dependence on private investment and foreign capital, elements that seemed increasingly reluctant to bet on the industrialisation of Mexico after taking into account the poor economic performance of the country since the early 1980s.

As a sign of discontent, these business groups began to mobilise politically in pursuit of a bigger say across the political system. Their main objective was to bring industrial policy back in. Nonetheless, the federal government paid no heed to industrial elites' petitions for some sort of State support or guidance within the new globalised context. When debating the pros and cons of entering into the NAFTA treaty in 1994, a handful of representatives of Mexico's bigger businesses asked Jaime Serra Puche, then Secretary of Commerce and Industrial Development, about the industrial policy to be expected from the federal government, to which he responded: "NAFTA is our industrial policy"; and before further questioning, he declared that an industrial policy, particularly a vertical one, was not viable within the new liberal economic model (Johnson, 1998, p. 137). A decade later, the paradigm of industrial policy in Mexico had become entrenched: its absence.

Due to this lack of industrial policies in the face of an economic opening, domestic industries began to be increasingly displaced by large TNCs

(Fouquet, 2007; Carrillo & Salinas, 2010). In the words of Moreno-Brid (2013), industrial policy became the "missing link" in Mexico's development since the end of the 20th century. After the 1994 crisis, moreover, regional disparities within Mexico deepened. As Hiskey (2005) illuminated, the first years after the 1994 crisis demonstrated the disparities in the subnational capacities to respond to the abandonment of the federal government in economic development-related policy areas. The more developed states of the centre and north of the country had capacities and infrastructures considerably superior to those of the southern states. The importance of this unevenness is further accentuated when one considers that a solid industrial infrastructure was essential to landing what appeared to be the only source of investment in the neoliberal model: foreign direct investment (FDI).

As the first decade of the 21st century was coming to an end, Mexico's federal government acknowledged that trade liberalisation had resulted in a considerable de-linkage of domestic industries from global productive chains; nevertheless, the federal government excluded any possibility of industrial subsidies or sectoral policies (Moreno-Brid, 2013). The adoption of the *maquiladora* model in Mexico, based on cheap labour and little or no added value from domestic industries, continued to take root in the country with adverse effects. During the two administrations of the far-right National Action Party (PAN) from 2000 to 2012, the dominant axiom in economic development was that "the best industrial policy was to have none at all" (Guajardo, 2014). Both administrations of the PAN emphasised instead the attraction of FDI as the main engine of economic development.

In parallel, the federal government's "abandonment" of the area of economic development (Trejo, 2017) would generate a "race to the bottom" below the State's centre (OECD, 2009). In the words of a former delegate of the federal Secretariat of Economy, this lack of coordination of a holistic industrial policy for the country and its states generated a "crude fight" for investments that still prevails in Mexico:

> The states are now free to fight to compete for investments and bring them to their territory. I think this is positive, it has of course its disadvantages, its problems, as it is that there is a crude fight between the states. And many times, when companies already decided between three states, they go for the highest bidder, and that means that the states exercise or invest significant resources in that: in buying a land, in urbanizing it, in bringing basic services between the municipality and the state to provide light, water, etc.

Due to these circumstances, regional inequalities worsened, and domestic industries were increasingly excluded from global value chains (Peters,

2000; Hiskey, 2005). In the new century, some states began to associate the negative effects of commercial deficits and de-linkage of domestic industries with the *maquiladora* or outsourcing model that had expanded after NAFTA. As a response, subnational governments began to formulate the first approximations towards sectoral industrial policies with an emphasis on added value, integration of domestic industries and the generation of higher-skilled jobs. In the long run, therefore, rather than seeing a complete State curtailment or an "eclipse of the state" (Evans, 1997) in terms of economic development, the developmental roles again expanded amid the newly empowered subnational actors.

In an effort to trace this rise of developmental policies across subnational platforms following Mexico's neoliberal turn, the cases of Nuevo León and Querétaro will illustrate the subnational deviation they represented in relation to the neoliberal policy regime. As these chapters will examine, the policy regimes pursued at the federal level and at the subnational level experienced a growing divergence – the federal level was increasingly neoliberal, whilst the subnational level played a more proactive or state-activist role.

The divergent policy regime that took shape at the subnational level thus resonates with the interscalar incompatibility that the previous theoretical chapters have underlined. The multilevel conjuncture of globalising, democratising and decentralising trends enabled subnational state actors to formulate their own response to the new paradigms that were reconfiguring the Mexican context. At the same time, the contrast between development policy regimes at the national and subnational levels echoes Polanyi's (1944) concept of the "double movement": a tendency to go back and forth between market-oriented and state-oriented models of development. The novelty that we are witnessing after the multilevel conjuncture, however, is the simultaneous characteristic in which this double movement is taking shape within different levels of the State. The following section will therefore make an effort to portray the policy transformation that took shape in Nuevo León after Mexico's trade liberalisation. First, however, I will provide a brief overview of the comparative method that was implemented to analyse these subnational strategies in Nuevo León and Querétaro.[1]

Scaling down industrial development: a subnational comparative method for Mexico

Throughout the empirical chapters, fieldwork which I undertook in Mexico will contribute in the examination of this more proactive role that the governments of Nuevo León and Querétaro have played since the turn of the century. The findings I will provide through these empirical chapters are based mainly on semi-structured interviews with both federal and sub-national economic development actors – such as federal delegates of the Secretariat of Economy, subnational secretaries and under-secretaries, and private sector actors involved in the states' economic development. Furthermore, other important primary sources on which I based my research were the subnational State Development Plans that I had the opportunity to examine in the archives of the state governments' offices and in the LLILAS Centre of the University of Texas.

What this research sought through its case study selection is the comparison of two Mexican states based on the Most Different Design System (MDDS) (see Landman, 2000). Nuevo León and Querétaro are two substantially different cases which achieved a similar end, in this case, an industrial transformation. It was thus considered that one of the main contributions this book could make was in showing how, despite substantial differences between these two Mexican states, the presence of specific variables enabled the policy transformation that eventually led to successful industrial projects.

Nuevo León is the 8th largest Mexican state in terms of population, and the 13th in terms of territory (out of a total of 32 federal entities). Nuevo León, furthermore, was the pioneering industrial state in Mexico, and since the beginning of the 20th century was considered the "industrial crown" of Mexico. At the end of the 19th century, its society was led by big, wealthy families of land-holders who eventually became the country's leading industrial families in the past century. In the late 19th century and the first decades of the 20th, Nuevo León experienced its first industrial transformation led by local political and economic elites.

In contrast, Querétaro is one of the smaller Mexican states. Located in Mexico's centre, it is the 27th state in terms of territory and the 21st in terms of population. During the 1950s, when Nuevo León was already the industrial leader in Mexico, Querétaro was still one of the poorest and most marginalised Mexican states, with a predominantly rural outlook. As of now, however, Querétaro usually comes up among the top three leaders regarding industrial activity in Mexico (INEGI, 2016; Márquez, 2015). Its first industrial transformation thus came during "Mexico's Miracle" (1940–1980), as the previous chapter explicated, in a substantially different timeframe and context than Nuevo León's first industrial transformation. Moreover, before its industrialisation, Querétaro's society was characterised by small *rancheros* (farmers) and merchants, and lacked the accumulation of pre-industrial capital needed for industrial transformation.

How, then, did these two substantially different states engage in a project of industrial transformation with similar rates of success? Were there any shared patterns or traits that could benefit from examination of these two subnational cases? Regarding the comparative framework, these are two of the guiding questions that this chapter intends to unravel. Accordingly, this research chose to compare these two subnational cases based on Snyder's subnational comparative method (2001) as well. As a starting point, I considered this method to be helpful for engaging with comparisons with "many variables, small N". Although industrialisation as a process encompasses a large number of variables, this subnational comparison has illuminated the common patterns and traits that were contributory to the success of these processes.

Thus, Table 4.1 is an effort to include the main variables that are usually considered in studies of industrialisation. Alexander Gerschenkron, for instance, emphasises the importance of "sizeable preindustrial accumulation of capital" (1962, p. 35), whilst Hirschman (1958, p. 53) also points to

Table 4.1 Comparative outlook between Nuevo León and Querétaro

Nuevo León	Querétaro
Geographic location	
State in the north-east	State in the central part of Mexico, north of Mexico's capital; part of the Bajío region
Type of industrialiser regarding its timing	
Pioneering state regarding industrialisation in Mexico	Late-comer regarding industrialisation
Size	
One of Mexico's bigger states: 64,156 km^2 (13th among Mexico's 32 states), with a population of around 5 million (8th)	Small state: 11,699 km^2 (27th in Mexico), with a population of around 2 million (21st in Mexico)
Timeframe of first industrial transformation	
End of the 19th century to beginning of the 20th century	Mid-20th century
Pre-industrial capital before first industrial transformation	
Abundance of pre-industrial capital	Absence of pre-industrial capital
Parties in government during the 21st century	
Prevalence of the PRI in the governor's seat; only once did it lose to the PAN, in 1997. In 2015, first gubernatorial election of an independent governor – meaning one without party affiliation.	Continuing alternation between the two main political parties (PRI and PAN) since political competition began in Mexico; PAN won in 1997 and in 2003; in 2009, PRI won the state back. In 2015, PAN again won the election.

Source: Author's elaboration.

the scarcity of pre-industrial capital as a traditional obstacle for underdeveloped countries. Gallup, Sachs, and Mellinger (1999), in contrast, point more emphatically towards the relevance of geography in a country's development or industrial outlook, while authors such as W. Brian Arthur (1994), in turn, highlight the relevance of timing in relation to industrialisation, with the concepts of increasing returns and path dependence at its centre.

The principal aim of my application of the MDDS method for Mexico's subnational cases of industrialisation is thus to highlight what I considered to be the main factors or "independent variables": the presence of both a vertical integration between the subnational and the federal government, achieved by governors' binding efforts, and a horizontal strategy which emphasised the institutionalisation of development at the subnational platform. It was thus as a result of this multilevel interaction that transforming institutions for industrialisation were put into place in these two subnational states – underscoring as well the importance of institutions with regards to economic development (see Acemoglu & Robinson, 2013; Hausmann, Rodrik, & Sabel, 2008).

However, I am not pretending to state that these vertical and horizontal strategies encompassing governors as binding agents, state-society collaborations and industrial policy continuity suffice for projects of industrial transformation, because other variables matter as well. In the case of Mexico, it seems farfetched to think of a rapid industrialisation in southern states such as Chiapas or Guerrero, considering Mexico's regional disparities or what Dávila, Kessel, and Levy (2002) call a "distortion of comparative advantages" to the detriment of the southern states of Mexico.

Rather, what this project acknowledges from the start is that, in the words of De Schweinitz (1964, p. 7), these independent variables were "necessary but not sufficient conditions". The dependent variable for my case studies was thus a structural transformation of the state's industry. As the following chapters will highlight, Querétaro's developmental policy regime provided the state with a new comparative advantage in a high-tech and emerging sector such as aeronautics (Secretaría de Economía, 2012); in Nuevo León, the developmental policy regime enhanced the state's transition to a "knowledge economy" based on high-tech sectors. Furthermore, with all intentions of being transparent, I also recognise the presence of a selection bias given the inherent character of the MDDS method considering I chose the cases based on the dependent variable (see Landman, 2000).

Accordingly, the differences listed in Table 4.1 helped me not only in discarding other variables as driving factors (geography, timeframe and accumulation of pre-industrial capital, among others), but also in highlighting the role of the aforementioned independent variables. Nonetheless, I do not intend to say that geography or the timing of the cases' industrial transformations did not matter; rather, one of my arguments is that vertical and horizontal strategies of institutionalisation which secured public policy continuity had the opportunity to exploit a favourable constellation of factors – be it geography, timing, political party affinity, state-society synergies, foreign or domestic capital, or alliances with other levels of government, to name a few.

Through this subnational comparison between Nuevo León and Querétaro, the present chapter explores the different impacts that the same national and even international context has had on subnational industrialisation, i.e. globalisation within Latin America and the liberalisation of Mexico's economy. Comparisons and contrasts are thus drawn from both case studies in order to highlight what can be considered the transforming factors in both cases: the presence of vertical integration between subnational and federal governments, and the consolidation of horizontal strategies of industrialisation based on state-society mechanisms, both of which eventually led to an industrial or structural transformation.

By implementing this comparative approach, this project is able to reach the three goals set by Skocpol and Somers for comparative-historical studies (in Collier, 1993, p. 108): firstly, examining the covariation or, in this case, subnational variation among the two cases in order to construe a causal analysis of industrial transformation; secondly, exposing how a particular set of models (the developmental policy regime, in this case) and concepts (e.g. interscalar incompatibility) "usefully illuminates these cases"; and thirdly, examining how different these cases are but, still, how they have managed to recreate "parallel processes of change" (e.g. industrial transformation). In the following section, this chapter will assess the process of policy transformation that was undertaken in the state of Nuevo León.

Vertical integration in Nuevo León: decentralising fiscal resources for subnational strategies

Across Latin America, the "lost decade" represented by the 1980s – with a heavy reliance on international financial institutions' structural adjustments and open market reforms – gave way to an "enhanced role for transnational capital" among the governments of those developing countries (Grugel & Riggirozzi, 2009, p. 5). In the particular case of Mexico, however, a large part of this "enhanced role" meant the displacement of indigenous capital and even a "race to the bottom" between competing subnational states.

In Nuevo León, to make matters worse, the 1980s had offered a bitter international experience for its enterprises. The oil boom at the end of the 1970s and beginning of the 1980s had propagated an irresponsible and ambitious expansion of the Monterrey Group's enterprises (Sánchez, 2007). In an effort to stabilise the country and gain these economic elites' confidence once more, President Miguel de la Madrid spent 788.246 billion pesos to rescue 44 enterprises of that group through the FICORCA (Exchange Risk Coverage Fund) project (Palacios, 2007, p. 231).

When President Carlos Salinas (1988–1994) entered his administration, the reinforced liberalism and eventual signing of NAFTA initially aggravated the circumstances of Nuevo León's entrepreneurs. With the aggravation of the trade deficit in Nuevo León, SMEs largely went bankrupt, and neighbouring states from the north, along with Bajío states such as Aguascalientes, Guanajuato and Querétaro, surpassed Nuevo León's industrial prowess (López, 2007, p. 81). According to a former Secretary of Economic Development of Nuevo León, during the presidencies of Vicente Fox and Felipe Calderón there had been a political "inertia" of converting the Bajío region into another industrial pole of Mexico, hinting at the fact that both presidents were born and made their political careers in the Bajío:

> During the previous federal administrations, there was a very strong inertia towards supporting the area of the Bajío, to strategically develop that pole. During ten years there was a very focused strategy to develop the Bajío area. That if that represents a political matter, well, I think it responds to a natural inertia. I believe that it is not particular to Mexico but to public policy and any system. However, that privilege or that approach to develop the area of the Bajío obviously diminished other entities of strategic resources, and the opportunity of landing strategic resources.

Furthermore, local enterprises from Nuevo León began to lose their competitiveness after NAFTA amid a higher presence of foreign capital, generating as well a higher dependence on TNCS and their capital (Fouquet, 2007, p. 135). Due to the predation of TNCs, the generalised demand that Mexican entrepreneurs made to Zedillo at the beginning of his administration (1994–2000) was to adopt once again an overarching industrial policy for the country's economic development, a request which, nonetheless, went unheeded (Luna, 1995, p. 88).

This was precisely the context within which Governor González Parás (2003–2009) arrived to take on the gubernatorial chair of Nuevo León. By then, Nuevo León's government was among the many subnational governments which recognised the need to fill the vacuum that the national government had traditionally occupied regarding industrial policy and economic development. To regain Nuevo León's industrial edge through subnational programmes and strategies as intended by Governor González, however, demanded a substantial amount of fiscal and financial resources – resources which had traditionally been centralised as part of Mexico's fiscal system.

Analysts of Mexico's political system (Díaz-Cayeros, 2006; Hernández, 2006; Ward & Rodríguez, 1999) have highlighted the centralisation of fiscal resources as one of the traditional imprints of Mexico's federal system during the 20th century. Even in comparison with other federal countries of Latin America, such as Brazil and Argentina, Mexico was usually considered as one of the most fiscally and politically centralised countries throughout the past century (see Eaton, 2004; Falleti, 2010). Nonetheless, the PRI's loss of the presidential chair in 2000 against the PAN would start to undo Mexico's traditional fiscal centralisation.

As analysed by Eaton (2004) across Latin America's federal countries, the intergovernmental relations between the president and state governors frequently become conflictual due to back and forth negotiations over fiscal resources. During these conflicts, governors have efficiently turned to legislators in the national congress for leverage whilst "pushing" for decentralisation of resources (Eaton, 2004, p. 61; see also Willis, Garman & Haggard, 1999). In the words of Eaton (2004), "governors in Argentina and Brazil have consistently used their leverage over national legislators as an asset that can help them compel the adoption of decentralization" (pp. 60–61).

This would eventually be the case of Mexico after the PRI lost the presidential chair for the first time in more than 70 years. As depicted by Hernández (2006), during President Fox's administration (2000–2006), the governors from the opposition parties – PRI and PRD (Party of the Democratic Revolution) – organised promptly through the CONAGO (National Commission of Governors) in an effort to acquire a bigger share of the country's revenue. The governors, in turn, expanded their negotiations with legislators from the PRI (including Senator Natividad González, who would soon be elected Nuevo León's governor) and PRD in the national congress, resulting in unprecedented fiscal decentralisation: in 2003, federal transfers to subnational governments rocketed, with the states set to receive 50% of the country's total income from oil sales (Hernández, 2006, p. 116).

Just to provide an idea of the vast increase in the states' treasuries, in 1996 the Mexican states' average expenditure amounted to a total of 4 billion pesos (Gutiérrez, 2013). In 2007, the state of Nuevo León alone registered a total income of 40.93 billion pesos (Gobierno NL, 2007, p. 175). According to Governor González, the main factors contributing to this exponential increase in the state's resources were the incorporation of revenues from oil sales and the recent tax reform, which also increased the federal government's transfer of resources. In the following years, Governor González and the rest of the PRI governors would use the CONAGO association to call for the first National Fiscal Convention, in which the decentralisation of fiscal resources would continue to be woven in favour of Mexico's intermediate level of government and away from the traditional stronghold that the national government used to have (Hernández, 2006).

Horizontal institutionalisation of Nuevo León's industrial policy

The main duty which Governor González took upon entering his administration was reinstating Nuevo León's past competitiveness and industrial edge. In this order of things, Nuevo León soon joined other subnational governments such as São Paulo and California (Ferreira, Jacobi, Rodríguez, Ward, & Wilson, 2008), which had proved particularly effective in exploiting their industrial tradition and their higher human capital resources towards enhanced competitiveness. In this sense, Governor González undertook the role of "binding agent" (Hirschman, 1958, p. 10) for Nuevo León's economic development by emphasising the coordination and cooperation of all state-society resources. He thus began a long path of industrial restructuring, much of which was realised through Evans' "midwifery role" (1995, pp. 13–14), which focused on inducing entrepreneurial groups to undertake investments and projects in more industrially challenging sectors.

In his administration's State Development Plan (Plan Estatal de Desarrollo), Governor González (Gobierno NL, 2004) declared, as one of his main goals, the repositioning of Nuevo León as a modern Mexican state with industrial and educational advantages within the new international context. To pursue this "repositioning", Governor González relied on the two main mechanisms which had first given Nuevo León its industrial edge a century ago.

First came the re-weaving of state-society synergies through the institutionalisation of coordinated efforts towards economic growth. This process was undertaken through a "triple helix" model – with the participation of state, academic and business sectors. This institutionalisation of public-private cooperation thus recalls the definition provided by Hausmann et al. (2008, p. 4) for "good" industrial policy in the new century: "institutional arrangements and practices that organize this (public-private) collaboration effectively" (see also Devlin & Moguillansky, 2009; Schneider, 2015). Secondly, there was the implementation of an ambitious set of fiscal and entrepreneurial incentives for businesses – tax exemptions, real estate donations, business and legal consultancy, economic donations and infrastructural enhancements, among others. Through these mechanisms, Governor González deployed an extensive array of incentives with the objective of, in the words of Hirschman (1958, p. 10), "maximising induced decision-making" for local and foreign investors.

Throughout his State Development Plan, Governor González placed clear emphasis on the state's initiative to forge state-society synergies towards economic growth. Therefore, the state government started to promote the association with the subnational state's universities and its business sector using a more inclusive and governance-oriented approach. The main project to achieve this, also decreed in the State Development Plan, was to consolidate the state's capital, Monterrey, as an "International City of Knowledge".

Accordingly, MTYCIC, as the project was later known, thus initially began as a rather open-ended project with four objectives: promoting technological development and the establishment of "knowledge" enterprises; projecting Nuevo León's high-quality education at an international level; developing the necessary urban infrastructure; and, as an axis for the state's economic development, assuring high competitiveness of both the private and public state sector (Gobierno NL, 2004).

MTYCIC was then supported through the governor's Law for the Foment of Knowledge-Based Development in Nuevo León in March 2004. Besides its core objective of generating knowledge-based development, the law's article 1 highlighted the "coordination between public, private and academic sectors" as the core principle in generating technological and scientific development. Through this law, the Council of Science and Technology for the State of Nuevo León was established, with a Council of Citizen Participation as its promoting and consultant body. This second council was composed of 14 councillors – including Nuevo León's Secretary of Economic Development, the Secretary of Education, the Head of Nuevo León's Corporation for Strategic Projects and 11 councillors representing the academic, scientific, social, cultural and entrepreneurial sectors.

This institutionalised framework of state-society relations promptly surpassed the expected progress for Governor González's initiatives. With additional support from the federal National Council of Science and Technology (CONACYT), just months after being published, the law and its synergistic mechanisms enabled the elaboration of a fund of 70 million pesos destined for productive and infrastructural investments with regards to MTYCIC (Armendáriz, 2004).

Soon after, the government's pending task was defining "the strategic areas of knowledge susceptible of achieving higher growth in the region", according to the State Development Plan (Gobierno NL, 2004, p. 158). Consequently, the strategic sectors to be promoted within this project were then defined between the government of Nuevo León and the three top universities from the region – Monterrey Tech, the Autonomous University of Nuevo León (UANL) and the University of Monterrey (UdeM).

The strategic areas were biotechnology, health, information technologies and telecommunications, advanced materials and mechatronics. Afterwards, these state-society coalitions devised the construction of an industrial park to host the project. The industrial and technological park – the Park of Research and Technology Innovation Park (PIIT) – was conceived by Nuevo León's Council of Science and Technology. This industrial park was located near Monterrey's international airport and consisted of 70 hectares. The first centres to commit investment expenditure to the industrial park were research centres from the UANL and CONACYT, set to be inaugurated in the first trimester of 2007. Likewise, research centres from Monterrey Tech, UdeM and the state's Association of Information Technology Enterprises, consisting of 42 enterprises, soon committed substantial investments to the PIIT; with regard to IT enterprises, the government donated 15,000 square metres of the park's real estate in return for an investment of around 100 million pesos.

Still, the total investment needed to habilitate the first 30 hectares of the PIIT seemed far away, as it was estimated at a billion pesos. Governor González, after seeing a positive response from the private and academic sectors, thus became convinced that the government's commitment had to be strengthened. In this line, Governor González formulated the Law for Fomenting Industry and Employment. Its main objective was to incentivise national and foreign investment in sectors with higher productivity and employment with high added value, and also to consolidate the state's competitiveness towards economic development and social welfare.

This law, in its article 3, defined an "incentive" as the "direct or indirect stimulus provided by the Executive Power of the State of Nuevo León to an investor, with the objective of facilitating the culmination of a direct investment". The Secretariat of Economic Development (SEDEC) was put in charge of implementing the provisions of this law. Among its core objectives of incentivising investments and competitiveness, the cited law likewise emphasised the promotion of associativity and collaboration of enterprises and research centres, "especially in the sectors defined as strategic, with the objective of consolidating the economic development of knowledge". Within these strategic sectors, Governor González and the participating agents of this council thus began promoting "clusters" or "entrepreneurial groupings" (*agrupamientos empresariales*).

Equally important were the investment incentives implemented by the administration of Governor González, which included the following: a discount of up to 95% in state taxes; economic donations to be destined for scholarships or the training of workers; construction of up to 100% of the infrastructure works promoting greenfield or brownfield investments or the donation of the economic resources required for their execution; donation of resources for the creation or improvement of public services; donation, sale, lease or trust of real estate for industrial projects; economic donations for the acquisition of real estate up to a maximum of 50%; economic donations of up to 100% of leasing contracts for a period of up to ten years; support in establishing linkages with local purveyors; and, finally, the undertaking of the related paperwork with municipal, state and federal authorities.

Through this framework of incentives, investment from local, national and international economic agents soon increased exponentially. Moreover, many of those new investments were accordingly established in the PIIT. Leading local and national enterprises such as Cemex, Alfa, Cydsa and Gamesa entered into negotiations with the SEDEC, PIIT and MTY-CIC authorities as they looked to obtain incentives and establish themselves within the PIIT (Milenio, 2006). TNCs also promptly entered into negotiations with the referred authorities, for example, Pepsi, Motorola, Schneider and AMD Technologies. Furthermore, to reinforce the support that the private sector of Nuevo León showed for this array of industrial policies, the Monterrey Group launched a capital private equity fund to promote and support innovation projects within the productive industries. At the beginning, the Monterrey Group contributed 15 million dollars while Nuevo León's government contributed 2 million dollars (Ramírez, 2007).

The success of these new developmental policies in Nuevo León began to crystallise during the second half of Governor González's administration. In that year (2007), the state of Nuevo León was the Mexican state with the highest percentage of productive investment within its programmable budget (Gobierno NL, 2007, p. 51; INEGI, 2016). The exports of two of the state's strategic sectors, automotive and household electronics, increased by 24% and 11.45% respectively (Gobierno NL, 2007, p. 38). Exports in general increased by 8 billion dollars, 6.5% more than in the same period of the preceding year; additionally, in 2007, FDI was 1.924 billion dollars, contributing to an increase of 36% in comparison to 2006 (Gobierno NL, 2007, p. 39). For 2008, Governor González made a clear statement reinforcing his administration's commitment to productive investments and industrial innovation by allocating 350 million pesos of the public budget towards the second PIIT phase (Vélez, 2008).

By the time the following gubernatorial administration began, Nuevo León once again had gained a leading place in Mexico's industrial development. The PRI had once again been elected for the 2009–2015 administration, but now the SEDEC took a more proactive role in consolidating the state's developmental policy regime. Within this proactive role, the cornerstone of the state's economic development guidelines was still the Law for Fomenting Investment and Employment, decreed by Governor González.

The MTYCIC had largely been absorbed by the remarkable success of the PIIT. But the overarching framework for promoting economic development within the region was the same: industrial incentives and a tripartite

Table 4.2 Top five Mexican states with regards to the ratio of activities with high competitiveness within their economies and their value added

State	Activities with high competitiveness (%)	Value added (%)
Nuevo León	65.0	76.4
Ciudad de México	64.6	60.9
Baja California	51.4	69.6
Sonora	50.7	72.8
Coahuila	50.0	69.0

Source: Author's elaboration based on data from Unger (2017).

collaboration between public, private and academic sectors. The main tool to achieve this triple helix was the state's economic "clusters", which were established in the economic sectors that Governor González and the academy had defined since the preceding State Development Plan.

According to a former Secretary of Economic Development during the administrations of both Governor González and Governor Medina, Nuevo León became the great pioneer in Mexico in terms of the "clusterisation" of the economy:

> Nuevo León was a pioneer in this subject of clusters. We began to group our state's industrial sectors into productive schemes that coincide with the clustering scheme that we have, which is I believe the model of successful economic development in Nuevo León – that model of virtuous partnership, of productive collaboration to generate best practices of academia, business and government, to create mechanisms that favor the economic environment of the sector. In other words, assuring that the piece of the pie stays in Nuevo León, and then we will figure out how that piece is distributed in our state.

In the case of Nuevo León's automotive cluster, for instance, the government gave an annual economic support of 3 million pesos and took charge of the lease for the cluster's offices in exchange for reports on activities – which could vary, depending on the case, from a monthly to a yearly basis (interviews, 2014). In this manner, the SEDEC of Nuevo León consolidated and sponsored development projects from clusters in the strategic sectors contemplated in the Law for Fomenting Investment and Employment: automotive, aeronautics, agro-industrial, biotechnology, household electronics, nanotechnology, information technologies, health services and housing construction.

Regarding SMEs, the SEDEC also formulated a specific programme to incentivise entrepreneurship and the internationalisation of this sector, which accompanies entrepreneurs from the very first step of creating their business image to the export of their products. This programme includes free training courses in accountability and financial management, and even orientation on the legal procedures to constitute their enterprises. In the words of the coordinator, the programme Hecho en Nuevo León (Made in Nuevo León) also emphasises commercial internationalisation:

> We give local SMEs specific training in exports. For companies that do not have the idea of what it is to export, but they already want to go out to other markets, and to associate with more mature companies. And they have investigated that they can be bought better abroad. And we take these companies to expositions across the border (to the United States). It is a very small contribution, but in this way, they become acquainted with the procedures required to export.

During the administration of Governor Medina (2009–2015), the developmental policies continued to show signs of success, with high-tech projects in several fields. A software programme to monitor an aeronautic pilot's mental activity was created; a chip to detect any illness in minutes was devised; and nanocomponents were invented for manufacturing processes including automotive and aeronautic components. Nuevo León's incubator for nanotechnology enterprises was rated among the international top ten (Buendía, 2014). Additionally, the first Mexican drone was designed and built, while prototypes for industry were printed in 3D, among other projects.

During the first five years of Governor Medina's administration, Nuevo León's economy grew by 27.3%, outpacing the country's growth of 17.9% by almost 10 points (Gobierno NL, 2014, p. 20; INEGI, 2016). The growth of manufacturing exports reached 11% of the country's total amount in 2015 (Gobierno NL, 2014). Its administration programme Hecho en Nuevo León supported more than 500 local enterprises in registering trademarks and attending international fairs, and it provided capacitation regarding exporting measures (Gobierno NL, 2014).

By the year 2013, Nuevo León had once again consolidated its competitiveness by having the most productive, diversified and competitive economy among Mexican states; furthermore, Nuevo León's productivity was supported on industrial activities with a highly skilled workforce, which explained why Nuevo León had the highest combined index of both labour productivity *and* average salaries among Mexican states (see Unger, 2017). Overall, the latter evidences a departure from the low-wage model that had taken root in Nuevo León (and Mexico in general) during the 1990s and the early 2000s through the *maquiladora* sector.

Table 4.3 Domains and instruments of Nuevo León's industrial policy (2003–2015)

Domain	Instruments
Economic signals and incentives	-Tax breaks
Scientific and technological innovation	-Scientific policies
	-High-tech lead projects
	-Funding of university research
	-Establishment of research centres
	-R&D subsidies and tax credits
Learning and improving technological capabilities	-Education and training policies
	-Foresight exercises (to detect Nuevo León's priorities)
	-Skills formation
	-International educational and research collaboration (collaboration with the University of Texas)
	-Incentives for FDI
Selective industry support	-Directed finance/subsidies
	-Provision of export support
Distribution of information	-Collective action mechanisms (in public-private councils)
	-Use of consultative forums
	-Use of business chambers
	-Encouragement of firm cooperation/ linkages
Improving productivity of forms and entrepreneurs	-Providing or subsidising management training
	-Monitoring and assistance for SMEs
	-Infrastructure, funding and management for incubators and cluster formation
	-Promotion of public-private partnerships
	-Upgrading of economic infrastructure

Source: Author's elaboration for Nuevo León's case based on the categorisation by Naudé (2010).

Conclusion

The government of Nuevo León knowingly developed practices from East Asian, European and Brazilian regions that had experienced great accomplishments – namely, the implementation of industrial parks and clusters. Furthermore, Governor González's efforts regarding industrial policy were more attuned to Brazil's "new developmentalism", rather than to Mexico's extended neoliberalism. Nuevo León's government thus became more pro-active in regaining its industrial edge, with an emphasis on public-private collaboration, productive investments, internationalisation, and incentives for industry and innovation.

In this context, the ongoing institutionalisation of Nuevo León's industrial policy also contributed to Governor González's strategies. In this particular aspect, Thelen's elaboration of the "institutional systems" (1999, p. 283) of political economy is deemed relevant. In the case of Nuevo León, its institutional system of industrial policy was strengthened through several platforms relating to its sub-systems: legal frameworks; public-private councils regarding industrial relations, investments and innovation; and also a greater reliance on the SEDEC as the organisation in charge of coordinating these policies, paralleling the role of East Asian Tigers' pilot agencies.

Further along the road, the horizontal institutionalisation of Nuevo León's developmental policies enhanced their maintenance and continuation during the following gubernatorial administration. As several officials from the state's SEDEC related, Governor Medina's administration continued to rely upon the same legal frameworks, cluster strategies and public-private councils that had been established by his predecessor, consolidating in this manner a continuity of policies that is often lacking in Mexico due to electoral turnovers.

Note

1 Excerpts of chapters 4 and 5 appeared in Tijerina, W. (2018). Desarrollismo subnacional para el nuevo siglo. *Problemas del desarrollo*, 49(192), 169–192. [Online]. Available at: www.revistas.unam.mx/index.php/pde/article/view/58827 [Accessed 15 February 2019].

References

Acemoglu, D., & Robinson, J. A. (2013). *Why nations fail: The origins of power, prosperity, and poverty*. New York: Broadway Business.

Armendáriz, E. (2004). Monterrey: Ciudad Internacional del Conocimiento. *Ciencia UANL, VII*(03), 389–398.

Arthur, W. B. (1994). *Increasing returns and path dependence in the economy*. Ann Arbor: University of Michigan Press.

Buendía, A. (2014, September 22). Nanoincubadora de NL, en top 10 mundial. *El Norte*.

Calva, J. L. (2010). Reforma económica para el crecimiento sostenido con equidad. *Economía UNAM, 7*(21), 15–36.

Carrillo, M. A. & Salinas, R. J. (2010). "Siglo XXI. Sectores industriales emergaentes en Querétaro". In *La ciencia, el desarrollo tecnológico y la innovación en Querétaro*. Querétaro: Consejo de Ciencia y Tecnología de Querétaro.

Collier, D. (1993). The comparative method. In A. W. Finifter (Ed.), *Political science: The state of the discipline II*. Washington, DC: American Political Science Association.

Dávila, E., Kessel, G., & Levy, S. (2002). El sur también existe: un ensayo sobre el desarrollo regional de México. *Economía Mexicana, XI*, 203–207.

De Schweinitz, K. (1964). *Industrialization and democracy: Economic Necessities and Political Possibilities*. New York: The Free Press.

Devlin, R., & Moguillansky, G. (2009). Alianzas público-privadas como estrategias nacionales de desarrollo a largo plazo. *Revista Cepal, 97*, 97–116.

Díaz-Cayeros, A. (2006). *Federalism, fiscal authority, and centralization in Latin America*. Cambridge: Cambridge University Press.

Eaton, K. (2004). *Politics beyond the capital: The design of subnational institutions in South America*. Stanford, CA: Stanford University Press.

Evans, P. (1995). *Embedded autonomy: States and industrial transformation*. Princeton, NJ: Princeton University Press.

Evans, P. (1997). The eclipse of the state? Reflections of stateness in an era of globalization. *World Politics, 50*(1).

Falleti, T. G. (2010). *Decentralization and subnational politics in Latin America*. Cambridge: Cambridge University Press.

Ferreira, M., Jacobi, P., Rodríguez, V., Ward, P., & Wilson, R. (2008). Intergovernmental relations and the subnational state: The decentralization of public policy making. In *Governance in the Americas: Decentralization, democracy, and subnational government in Brazil, Mexico, and the USA*. Notre Dame: University of Notre Dame Press.

Fouquet, A. (2007). La industria maquiladora en Monterrey: Una actividad marginal pero reveladora de los cambios y tendencias económicas. In *Nuevo León en el Siglo XX. Apertura y globalización: De la crisis de 1982 al fin de siglo*. Monterrey: Fondo Editorial Nuevo León.

Gallup, J. L., Sachs, J. D., & Mellinger, A. D. (1999). Geography and economic development. *International Regional Science Review, 22*(2), 179–232.

Gerschenkron, A. (1962). *Economic backwardness in historical perspective*. Cambridge, MA: Belknap Press of Harvard University Press.

Gobierno del Estado de Nuevo León (Gobierno NL). (2004). Plan Estatal de Desarrollo. Monterrey: Gobierno del Estado de Nuevo León.

Gobierno del Estado de Nuevo León (Gobierno NL). (2007). Cuarto Informe de Gobierno del Estado de Nuevo León. Monterrey: Gobierno del Estado de Nuevo León.

Gobierno del Estado de Nuevo León (Gobierno NL). (2014). Quinto Informe de Gobierno del Estado de Nuevo León. Monterrey: Gobierno del Estado de Nuevo León.

Grugel, J., & Riggirozzi, P. (2009). The end of the embrace? Neoliberalism and alternatives to neoliberalism in Latin America. In J. Grugel & P. Riggirozzi (Eds.), *Governance after neoliberalism in Latin America* (pp. 1–23). London: Palgrave Macmillan.

Guajardo, I. (2014). *Discurso en la Reunión Anual de Industriales*. México: Secretaría de Economía.

Gutiérrez, S. E. (2007). Treinta años de vida política en Nuevo León. A vuelo de memoria, 1973–2003. In *Nuevo León en el Siglo XX. Apertura y globalización: De la crisis de 1982 al fin de siglo*. Monterrey: Fondo Editorial de Nuevo León.

Gutiérrez, P. C. (2013). El poder de los gobernadores en México 2001–2012: límites institucionales y políticos a nivel subnacional. México: Facultad Latinoamericana de Ciencias Sociales (FLACSO).

Hausmann, R., Rodrik, D., & Sabel, C. (2008). Reconfiguring industrial policy: A framework with an application to South Africa. Cambridge, MA: Harvard University.

Hernández, R. (2006). La disputa por el presupuesto federal. Presidencialismo y gobiernos estatales en México. *Foro Internacional, 183*(XLVI), 103–121.

Hirschman, A. O. (1958). *The strategy of economic development.* New Haven, CT: Yale University Press.

Hiskey, J. T. (2005). The political economy of subnational economic recovery in Mexico. *Latin American Research Review, 40*(1), 30–55.

Instituto Nacional de Estadística y Geografía (INEGI) (2016). Cuentas nacionales. Retrieved from www.inegi.org.mx/est/contenidos/proyectos/cn/.México

Johnson, K. (1998). Business-government relations in Mexico since 1990: NAFTA, economic crisis, and the reorganization of business interests. In R. Roett (Ed.), *Mexico's private sector: Recent history, future challenges.* Boulder, CO: Lynne Rienner Publishers.

Landman, T. (2000). *Issues and methods in comparative politics: An introduction.* London: Routledge Press.

López, V. (2007). De lo local a lo global. La experiencia de Nuevo León en la globalización. In *Nuevo León en el Siglo XX. Apertura y globalización: De la crisis de 1982 al fin de siglo.* Monterrey: Fondo Editorial de Nuevo León.

Luna, M. (1995). Entrepreneurial interests and political action in Mexico: Facing the demands of economic modernization. In R. Roett (Ed.), *The challenge of institutional reform in Mexico.* Boulder, CO: Lynne Rienner Publishers.

Márquez, D. (2015, November 2). Reporte económico de entidades. *La Jornada.*

Milenio (12 September 2006). El Parque de Innovación e Investigación Tecnológica albergará 42 empresas. *Milenio Diario.*

Moreno-Brid, J. C. (2013). Industrial policy: A missing link in Mexico's quest for export-led growth. *Latin American Policy, 4*(2), 216–237.

Naudé, W. (2010). *Industrial policy: Old and new issues (No. 2010, 106).* Working paper//World Institute for Development Economics Research.

Organisation for Economic Co-operation and Development (OECD) (2009). *Reviews of Regional Innovation: 15 Mexican States.*

Palacios, L. (2007). Consolidación corporativa y crisis económica en Monterrey, 1970–1982. In *Nuevo León en el Siglo XX. La industrialización: del segundo auge industrial a la crisis de 1982.* Monterrey: Fondo Editorial Nuevo León.

Panizza, F. (2009). *Contemporary Latin America: Development and democracy beyond the Washington consensus.* London: Zed Books.

Peters, E. D. (2000). *Polarizing Mexico: The impact of liberalization strategy.* Boulder, CO: Lynne Rienner Publishers.

Polanyi, K. (1944). *The great transformation: Economic and political origins of our time.* New York, NY: Farrar & Rinehart.

Ramírez, M. (2007, July 5). 'Grupo de los 10' apoyará proyectos de innovación de empresas. *El Norte.*

Sánchez, V. (2007). Los empresarios de Monterrey en la transición mexicana a la democracia. In *Nuevo León en el Siglo XX. La industrialización: del segundo auge industrial a la crisis de 1982.* Monterrey: Fondo Editorial de Nuevo León.

Schneider, B. R. (2015). *Designing industrial policy in Latin America: Business-state relations and the new developmentalism.* New York, NY: Palgrave Macmillan.

Secretaría de Economía (2012). *Industria Aeronáutica en México.* México: Gobierno Federal.

Snyder, R. (2001). Scaling down: The subnational comparative method. *Studies in Comparative International Development, 36*(1), 93–110.

Thelen, K. (1999). Historical institutionalism in comparative politics. *Annual Review of Political Science, 2*(1), 369–404.

Trejo, A. (2017). Crecimiento económico e industrialización en la Agenda 2030: perspectivas para México. *Problemas del Desarrollo. Revista Latinoamericana de Economía, 46*(188).

Unger, K. (2017). Evolución de la competitividad de las entidades federativas mexicanas en el siglo XXI. ¿Quién gana o pierde? *El trimestre económico, 84*(335), 645–679.

Vélez, J. M. (2008, Enero 12). Presupuesto 2008: Iniciará parque fase dos. *Milenio DIario.*

Ward, P. M., & Rodríguez, V. E. (1999). *New federalism and state government in Mexico: Bringing the states back in.* Austin: University of Texas Press.

Whitehead, L. (2006). *Latin America: A new interpretation.* New York: Springer.

Willis, E., Garman, C., & Haggard, S. (1999). The politics of decentralization in Latin America. *Latin American Research Review,* 7–56.

5 Subnational strategies after Mexico's trade liberalisation

Querétaro

Introduction

By the mid-1980s, the fracture in state-business relations in Mexico was one of the factors precipitating the end of Mexico's national drive towards industrialisation (Erfani, 1995). The ISI project was shut down amid a failed transition to its more complicated phase – the indigenous and competitive production of capital goods. The country's 1985 entrance to the GATT (General Agreement on Tariffs and Trade) mechanism served the administration of de la Madrid (1982–1988) as a "point of no return" for Mexico's new outward orientation. This neoliberal shift, though highly lobbied for by some economic elites, was soon resented across Mexico's businesses and industries (Johnson, 1998). The rising industrial niche that had been consolidated in Querétaro was no exception in the struggle against the new challenges of a more open economy.

From the 1940s up to the end of the Mexican Miracle in 1982, Querétaro had been transformed from a rural economy into one of Mexico's leading industrial entities. In the 1960s, during the administration of President López Mateos, consolidating the auto industry was seen as the next step in Mexico's industrialisation. However, the Mexican state's negotiations with the big automotive TNCs had been rather ineffective, giving the latter free entry to local production without any requirements for national content, at a time when Brazil and Argentina were threatening to gain an early advantage in this sector (Bennett & Sharpe, 1986).

A bit later, nonetheless, Mexico's Consejo de Fomento y Coordinación de la Producción Nacional placed emphasis on integrating local industry into the automotive sector, which the federal government answered by launching a decree which required a minimum of 60% of national content (Miranda, 2005, pp. 378–379). Within this timeframe, therefore, the growing ICA Group of Querétaro exploited the industrial conjuncture by entering into a joint venture with a US firm, Clark Enterprises, and thus establishing Tremec – an automotive enterprise.

By the end of the 1960s, Tremec was consolidated as one of the continent's leading producers of automotive transmissions, as it was able to enter into negotiations with the headquarters of Ford, eventually becoming one of the TNC's main suppliers of transmission parts (Miranda, 2005, p. 381). The success of Querétaro's Tremec eventually attracted other joint ventures until Querétaro was transformed into an industrial hub of automotive machinery.

Even amid the slow-down of Mexico's industrial miracle, Querétaro went from being the 19th Mexican state in 1970 to the 13th in 1980, in terms of industrial manufacturing growth (INEGI, 1986, p. 11). Moreover, by the end of the 1980s, Querétaro had ten industrial parks across its territory, which served as platforms to incentivise its industry (González & Osorio, 2000). As examined in the previous chapter, the industrial policies devised by Querétaro's government triggered the impressive transformation of a rather backward Mexican state in terms of industry. From the 1960s to the 1970s, through negotiations with either national industrialists (as in the ICA Group) or TNCs (as in Kellogg's or Massey Ferguson), Querétaro soon positioned itself as one of the leading states in sectors such as auto parts, machinery and steel-works.

But the end of Mexico's national industrialisation and the opening up of its economy shook Querétaro's industrial future. Many of the restrictions which Mexico had put on foreign investment as a way to trigger domestic industrialisation, and which had been strengthened through President Echeverría's Secretariat of Industry, were dismantled through the country's accession to the GATT. Moreover, the dismissal of trade protections and vertical subsidies left domestic industries standing mostly alone against international competitors. Given this, Querétaro's industrial efforts again had to be rethought in order to survive the new globalised competition.

Following the signing of NAFTA in 1994, the automotive sector, more than any other sector in Mexico, eventually set the tone for Mexico's development in the new century. The three bigger automotive TNCs – Chrysler, Ford and General Motors – began expanding their production facilities within Mexico, in accordance with the newly globalised trends of automotive production set by the rising East Asian firms (Daville-Landero, 2012). With the federal government's emphasis on attracting FDI as a surrogate for productive investments and industrial policy, landing investments from these big automotive TNCs seemed the next logical step for the new century's industrialisation. However, it was Querétaro's bigger neighbouring states which were landing these big TNCs' investments – Guanajuato, Aguascalientes, Puebla and Estado de Mexico – in what soon was characterised as a "race to the bottom" between states (OECD, 2009). Moreover, the lack of any federal-led coordination or policy regarding FDI accentuated this "race to the bottom" (interviews, 2015).

This orientation was most evident during the 1990s and the first decade of the 2000s, as two successive governors centred Querétaro's industrial policy on directing FDI towards the *maquila* sector (Carrillo & Salinas, 2010). Thus, the emphasis of Querétaro's government was no longer to rely on local entrepreneurship, competitiveness or innovation; rather, the focus became about attracting foreign enterprises with intensive workforce (*mano de obra*) requirements. According to Carrillo and Salinas (2010, p. 343), the initial consequences of this outward orientation in Querétaro were "the breaking of productive chains, a deficit in trade balance, the scarce contribution of the manufacturing sector to employment, the downfall of productive investments, a *tertiarisation* (of Querétaro's economy) and the uncontrolled growth of its informal sector".

Indeed, when Querétaro's second successive PAN governor, Francisco Garrido, entered his administration (2003–2009), Querétaro's industrial landscape was far from promising. Foreign industrial firms from the United States and Japan had largely displaced local producers from both local and global productive chains (Daville-Landero, 2012). Likewise, Querétaro's trade deficit had grown to 799.5 million dollars just during the year 2004 (SEDESU, 2005).

As witnessed in other Third World countries (Evans, 1995), the dismantling of Mexico's ISI greenhouse had gradually eroded productive chains and local suppliers. To counter the negative effects of the low-linked *maquila* sector and the displacement of local industry by the bigger TNCs, the administration of Governor Francisco Garrido (2003–2009) once more underscored the importance of strengthening Querétaro's local industry and creating higher-quality employment. Accordingly, the state government was emphatic in shifting its industrial focus away from the *maquila* sector, declaring it an unviable option for sustainable growth in Querétaro.

It was ultimately the upcoming aeronautic sector which would provide Querétaro with an industrial edge. In parallel to re-consolidating their automotive industry once again throughout the first decades of the 21st century, Querétaro's governments had been emphatic in building a new comparative advantage through the emerging aeronautic sector. Eventually, the automotive sector would be used by Querétaro's officials to upgrade local industries into the aeronautic sector. This project of industrialisation, however, exacted considerable efforts of vertical integration from both the public and private sectors of Querétaro.

Vertical integration: getting financial support for an emerging sector

Given the alternation in Mexico's presidential chair and the arrival of the PAN in Los Pinos (the presidential house), the country seemed ever more divided and fragmented in its efforts towards economic development. Some proposals by President Fox (2000–2006) regarding industrial policy mentioned the importance of sectoral initiatives but soon turned out to be mainly rhetoric, whilst the attraction of FDI became the overarching emphasis (Moreno-Brid, Santamaría, & Valdivia, 2005, p. 1103). However, some "political inertias" or "favouritisms" were being put in motion by President Fox regarding the attraction of FDI, as already reviewed in the previous chapter.

Subnational associations eventually rose as a counterbalance to this perceived show of favouritism. Firstly, the CONAGO began to question this perceived favouritism towards the Bajío; shortly afterwards, this effort was joined by the Mexican Association of Economic Development Secretaries (AMSDE) (interviews, 2015). The opposition within the CONAGO and AMSDE, however, was not the turning point for Querétaro's industry; rather, the issue lay with Querétaro's experienced implementation of mutually empowering relations between state and business, and their capacity to build a collaborative alliance with the presidential administration of President Fox.

One of President Fox's (2000–2006) crudest conflicts proved to be the deciding opportunity for Querétaro's industrial upgrading: the attempt to construct Mexico City's next international airport. On 22 October 2001, President Fox decreed the expropriation of 5,391 hectares near Mexico City to resolve the increasing saturation of the city's international airport. The peasants who owned the expropriated lands, however, proved an insurmountable obstacle to President Fox's initiative as they denounced what they saw as unjust compensation. After continuous mobilisation, legal remedies, road blockages and confrontations with federal police that went on for almost a year, these peasants managed to obtain President Fox's retraction of the initiated expropriations and related projects in August 2002 (Díaz, 2014).

This frustrated initiative, however, was seen as an opportunity in another jurisdiction: Querétaro. Governor Loyola (1997–2003), also from the PAN, had the same problem in Querétaro, as its international airport was saturated and mostly outdated. His project for a new airport counted nonetheless on support from the state's leading industrialists and generalised consent from the citizenry. This joint initiative of the governor and industrialists was then presented to President Fox as a temporary solution for the failed attempts at constructing Mexico City's new airport. The project quickly garnered the President's unconditional support as it was also devised to alleviate part of Mexico City's air traffic problem, and presidential support eventually crystallised in the commitment to finance 30% of the airport's costs (Molinari, 2004).

Accordingly, when President Fox's birthday neared in 2003, Governor Loyola went as far as saying that the construction of Querétaro's international airport would be finished on 2 July 2003, the same day as the President's birthday. In the words of Governor Garrido, Querétaro's international airport would be a "good gift" for the President (Crónica, 2003). When that date came, President Fox arrived at Querétaro's new international airport, though it was still far from finished, accompanied by Querétaro's governor. Querétaro's COPARMEX (Confederation of Mexican Employers) industrialists, likewise, welcomed the President with a birthday cake in the shape of an airport, even with miniature control towers and airplanes (Becerril & Chávez, 2003).

The proximity of the elections for Querétaro's gubernatorial chair and the local legislature garnered accusations against President Fox from the media and the PRI, who stated that the President was "promoting" activities of the PAN governor. The President, nonetheless, dismissed these allegations, answering that he had simply flown to Querétaro to have lunch at Querétaro's COPARMEX chamber and discuss the state's opportunities. At the same time, he complimented Querétaro's "great dynamism" and described how Querétaro was the second leader among Mexican states regarding employment in that same year (Becerril & Chávez, 2003).

What was left behind closed doors, nonetheless, was the latent possibility of redrawing Mexico's next leading economic sector with an important role for Querétaro. Due to Mexico's exponential growth in the automotive sector over the preceding decades and its similar consolidation in the field of electronics – though both led mostly by TNC capital – the aeronautic sector seemed like the next challenging arena for development through the attraction of FDI. By 2004, when FDI from interested aeronautic TNCs seemed up for grabs in Mexico, the global sales in the aeronautic sector were around 450 billion dollars (Secretaría de Economía, 2012): quite an alluring pie of profits.

In high-technology sectors, with substantial barriers to entry and a dominance of TNCs, the Third World's path towards a comparative advantage has generally implied alliances or negotiations between States and TNCs (Evans, 1995). This is even more so in today's increasingly internationalised context, with Mexico continuing to position FDI attraction as one of its main industrial policy pillars. Therefore, attracting and convincing the big TNCs – such as Bombardier, Airbus, Honeywell and Boeing – into local production in Mexico seemed like the next logical step.

Querétaro, which had been dismissed by all preceding TNC automotive assembly plants on Mexican soil, was thus looking to seize the opportunity to construct a comparative advantage in the aeronautic sector through using an aeronautic assembly plant as an "anchor enterprise". This would bring about a comparative advantage, not only in an international context, but even more so with regards to the national "race to the bottom" as other states would certainly offer aggressive incentives – tax exemptions, economic resources and real estate – to land this type of investment.

In the words of a former Vice-President of Querétaro's CAINTRA (Chamber for the Transformative Industry), gaining the first step in what seemed to be Mexico's next dynamic sector was all about "having the tortillas ready" and convincing President Fox about it. In other words, the state-capital synergies in Querétaro presented their case to President Fox as the appropriate host state, having the human capital, commitment and infrastructure to develop the aeronautic sector. Correspondingly, when the aeronautic TNC Bombardier announced its intentions to establish an assembly plant in Mexico in 2006, Querétaro came out on top as the preferred location.

The main factors in Bombardier's decision were Querétaro's geographical location, its industrial infrastructure, its expertise in the automotive sector and, first and foremost, the existence of trained human capital – a commitment which was strengthened with Querétaro's launch of its National Aeronautic University at Querétaro (UNAQ) in 2007. This collaboration of Querétaro's government with both the academic and the private sectors has thus been key in shaping this emerging industry for the state, according to the former Vice-President of Querétaro's CAINTRA:

> It helps a lot. An example is the aeronautical sector which has had a boom in the last eight years in Querétaro. What's going on? The aeronautical industry committed itself to investing in Querétaro. What are the challenges? Well, where do we get, first, skilled labour? And manpower is about all its levels: senior management, middle managers, technical, engineering and operators. So here, that example (of collaboration between the three sectors) has helped us a lot because there was a need on the part of the industry. And academia realised this. So then the state government, obviously in coordination with the municipalities, took to the task of providing skilled labour, to such level that we inaugurated the National Aeronautic University at Querétaro (UAQ). What the UNAQ wants to do is to assure that the aeronautical cluster is nourished by the local workforce so that the investments keep working.

Thus, in parallel to Querétaro's efforts to become an ally in the eyes of the President, the subnational government formulated industrial policies which emphasised public-private collaboration and technological upgrading in order to consolidate the state's competitiveness – as the following section will detail.

Horizontal institutionalisation of Querétaro's industrial policy

To tackle the commercial deficits that Querétaro had at the beginning of the 21st century, Querétaro's Secretariat of Sustainable Development (SEDESU) deployed strategies and programmes oriented towards a global integration of the state's local automotive industry. Given that Querétaro could not land a TNC assembly plant, the government's challenge was to consolidate its industry on the back of the state's existing expertise: mainly automotive transmissions. Since Governor Garrido's administration (2004–2009), the SEDESU's Under-Secretariat of Economic Development had begun to put in place programmes and initiatives to upgrade the state's industry. Along these lines, Querétaro's Under-Secretariat of Economic Development very much paralleled the "husbandry" role portrayed by Evans (1995, p. 140) in other Third World countries, with a specific emphasis on increasing or strengthening the capacities of local industries amid international competition in high-technology sectors.

As related by an official of the aforementioned under-secretariat, this bureaucratic unit began holding regular consultations between big automotive TNCs and local industries to integrate Querétaro's domestic businesses once again into the supply chain, along with training programmes for its human capital and certification programmes for automotive processes. This official, the Director of Supply Chains in Querétaro's Under-Secretariat of Economic Development, related the following:

> We opted instead to consolidate the supply base. We were reviewing investments in recent days: we have 74 Tier 1 companies, auto parts manufacturers, and that has contributed in developing the supply chain. In Querétaro, since 1963, we had the first company in the automotive sector and since then it has been consolidating that vocation for the automotive sector. First, going through metal-mechanical processes merely, with a high ratio of labour-intensive activities in assembly, and little by little we have been migrating to processes of higher technology in the sector.

The automotive sector, with a gradual but steady upgrading of its local industry, seemed once again like a consolidated sector in Querétaro by the end of the 21st century's first decade. Little by little, local suppliers began to upgrade their industrial capabilities. Following the account cited above by the SEDESU's official, this industrial upgrading was consolidated when local industries began migrating from more labour-intensive metal-mechanical products to more technologically demanding processes such as plastic injections, basic electronic parts and, more recently, the entire information and electronic equipment required by automobiles. The positive results were eventually felt in Querétaro's near trade balance in the automotive sector for 2009 (SEDESU, 2010).

The challenge, nonetheless, was to overcome Querétaro's increasing commercial deficit in other sectors of the economy through local production and manufacturing in sectors of higher technology. At the end of 2009, Querétaro's trade deficit had catapulted to 2,150.7 million dollars, more than tripling the deficit at the start of Governor Garrido's administration (SEDESU, 2010, p. 167). Nevertheless, two sectors presented themselves as silver linings: the automotive sector, with a trade deficit of only 3.7 million dollars, and 1,399.4 million dollars in total exports (SEDESU, 2010, p. 168), along with the promising aeronautic sector, which began attracting considerable national and international investments.

The consolidation of Querétaro's economic development in the new century, however, was still far from accomplished. When the administration of Governor José Calzada (2009–2015) began, the rising participation of local industry in the automotive sector and the arrival of the aeronautic company Bombardier were two good stepping stones to growth, but a local context of worsening trade deficits prevailed. Indeed, Querétaro's trade deficit in the manufacturing industry had increased more than 50%, going from 1,947 million dollars in 2005 to 2,925 million dollars in 2008 (Gobierno Querétaro, 2010).

Moreover, bureaucratic and administrative interruptions loomed once more over Mexico's economic development: Governor Calzada was from the PRI, whilst the previous two governors had been from the PAN. As portrayed by Byung Kook (1987), the lack of a meritocratic bureaucracy in Mexico has proven to be an obstacle to its economic development, in stark contrast to Korea's career-minded bureaucracy. In the new decentralised context in Mexico, the same perils were reflected in subnational administrations, including bureaucracies that did not require exams for entry and lacked meritocratic traditions. Every six years, changes in gubernatorial administrations' public servants take place across Mexican states with harsh effects on subnational projects.

Governor Calzada, nonetheless, put political colours aside by leaving the past administration's SEDESU team untouched. "Continuity" became thus one of the central pillars of Querétaro's reinforced industrialisation. Querétaro's former Under-Secretary of Economic Development highlighted the following:

> Look, I'll tell you how we're working here in Querétaro. Our government is from the PRI. But Querétaro is a state that has had a lot of party alternation: the two previous gubernatorial administrations were from the PAN, and before that, from the PRI. Still, within the state, there has been an emphasis on continuity and, in fact, it is one of the recipes for success in Querétaro: despite the change of parties, successful projects have continued, and even the Secretariat's team has continued mostly without modifications, as is the case of my boss, the Secretary

of Sustainable Development, who is still at the head of the Secretariat despite party alternation in the last gubernatorial election.

Leaving the same team within the Under-Secretariat of Economic Development proved to be key, yielding a total of 18 years of continuity. Programmes on enhancing backward linkages in Querétaro's industry were continued through the guidance of the same team who had first put them in place, along with training programmes for industries' human capital and certification programmes for local suppliers in Querétaro's more challenging sectors, such as information technology and the automotive and aeronautic sectors. As a sidenote, likewise, a former official of Querétaro's Under-Secretariat of Economic Development – after jokingly asking whether his name would be published or not – emphasised how federal support increased when they had, once again, a governor and a president from the same political party. "We are receiving much more federal resources with the new presidential administration. That's a fact!" he stated emphatically.

Now the focus on continuity, however, was not the only merit of Governor Calzada's State Development Plan, as he also put in place sectoral strategies of development – distinguishing between "consolidated" and "emerging" sectors – and aimed to strengthen state-society synergies through the "clusterisation" experiences pioneered by Nuevo León.

According to Querétaro's former Director of Supply Chains, dividing industrial sectors between "consolidated" and "emerging" sometimes led to blurred lines – especially in the aeronautic sector:

> First, for consolidated sectors we consider the contribution they have in the state: jobs, generation of foreign currency, and level of exports that they have. For the emerging sectors we consider obviously what one sees of potential growth. For example, the aeronautical sector is in that thin line between consolidated and emerging. It could be "consolidated" because it is already settled in our state, but I see it more as "emerging" because if today we see the type of components that are being developed in Mexico compared to what the aviation industry represents, we are still very limited. And that the window of growth looking forward is precisely what we want. Even more once you get to know the number of orders for aircrafts already in place in the market for the next ten years.

The automotive industry was clearly a consolidated sector, given its already historic tradition in Querétaro and the fact that it represented between 10% and 11% of the state's GDP. The electronic (*electrodomésticos*) and agro-industrial sectors were also defined as a consolidated sector considering, likewise, the already historic arrival of Singer and Kellogg's in the 1950s and 1960s, plus the subsequent linkages that formed around them. In between "emerging" and "consolidated" was therefore the aeronautic sector, which in the words of the same official could belong to either of the two considering its established presence in the state by 2015. This official, however, positioned it as an emerging sector given the pending tasks of further integrating local industry into its more challenging productive chains – largely dominated by TNCS such as Bombardier, Safran, Eurocopter and Aernnova, among others.

Along these lines, the Under-Secretariat of Economic Development continued developing an interesting strategy. In the first case, Querétaro's industrial strategies had been emphatic in attracting TNCs to start up the aeronautic sector in the state with incentives regarding real estate (Querétaro's Aeronautic Park within its international airport) and human capital facilities (through the establishment of Mexico's first aeronautic university). At the same time, industrial policies were kept in place in Querétaro's consolidated sectors through the same programmes of productive chains and certifications, though also with attempts to avoid lower-return activities.

According to Querétaro's former Under-Secretary of Economic Development, the objective of Querétaro's 2009–2015 administration was to upgrade Querétaro's industry towards activities of higher value. In consolidated sectors, such as the automotive, this usually meant multiplying industrial linkages between the Tier 3 enterprises and up-and-coming local producers – a strategy which was supported through the implementation of the "cluster" strategies first implemented in Nuevo León.

To promote the state's exports, likewise, a monitoring project for Querétaro's local industries, the Sistema de Comercio Exterior (COMEXQRO), was also put in place to identify opportunities occurring in the related productive chains with the objective of import substitution (SEDESU, 2005, p. 137). Within these policies, further emphasis on coordinating the state of Querétaro with federal programmes to promote exports was undertaken – for example, PITEX (Programme for Temporal Imports to Produce Exports), for exemptions on provisional imports, and ALTEX (Programme for Highly Exporting Enterprises), for enterprises with high export volumes.

The governors' initiative to attract FDI in the aeronautic sector led the SEDESU to numerous "commercial missions" around the globe such as to Detroit, Cincinnati and Berlin or promotional visits to cities, enterprises and ministries in Spain, Italy, France and Canada (Gobierno Querétaro, 2014). By 2014, Querétaro had been consolidated as the main recipient of aeronautic FDI with 48.4% of the national pie, followed in second place by Baja California, with a distant 12.5% (Torres, 2015). In the words of Querétaro's former Under-Secretary of Economic Development, landing productive investments was achieved by the secretariat's international promotion of the state:

> We do international promotion mostly in our strategic sectors, particularly in consolidated sectors such as automotive and aerospace. And we have sought to launch emerging sectors in particular here with information and communication technologies, and some health, food and biotechnology issues. We participate in fairs, in commercial missions abroad to promote our state. And our main job is to work with investor prospects by helping them, in a first stage, to get to know our region, and then to work on the business model that brings the company to Querétaro.

Likewise, consolidating a leading infrastructural space for the up-and-coming aeronautic sector was promoted as both an incentive and evidence of Querétaro's commitment to the sector. After the TNC Bombardier committed to investing more than 200 million dollars to establish in Querétaro in 2007, the state government created a public trust to further develop the sector. This trust – through ties with the TNC and Querétaro's private and academic sector – was kick-started with the state government donating 78 hectares within Querétaro's international airport to establish an Aeronautic Industrial Park. Moreover, within this industrial park, the state government invested 400 million pesos in Mexico's first aeronautic university – the UNAQ (Álvarez, 2007).

Then, through its Programa de Desarrollo de Proveedores Aeronáuticos (Programme for Development of Aeronautic Suppliers), the Under-Secretariat of Economic Development played a midwifery role with established local industries, generally in the automotive or electronic household sectors, inviting them to upgrade into the more challenging aeronautic sector whilst providing them with certification programmes and economic incentives (Carrillo & Salinas, 2010).

By 2009, 14 local enterprises had managed to complete a two-phase certification programme from the Under-Secretariat of Economic Development (Carrillo & Salinas, 2010). At the beginning of 2014, Querétaro had become renowned as "the only Mexican state able to start up an aeronautic industry of local capital" with 11 local enterprises as direct suppliers of the bigger TNCs or as independent exporters (Flores, 2014). According to SEDESU Secretary Marcelo López, in the past, these enterprises had dedicated their activities to the automotive and electronic household sectors until upgrading to the aeronautic sector. Consolidating local enterprises was thus a main objective of the SEDESU Secretariat. In the words of its Secretary, "if we

Table 5.1 Domains and instruments of Querétaro's industrial policy (2003–2015)

Domain	Instruments
Economic signals and incentives	-Tax breaks
Scientific and technological innovation	-Scientific policies
	-High-tech lead projects
	-Funding of university research
	-Establishment of research centres
	-R&D subsidies and tax credits
Learning and improving technological capabilities	-Education and training policies
	-Foresight exercises (defining Querétaro's "emerging sectors")
	-Skills formation
	-Incentives for FDI
Selective industry support	-Directed finance/subsidies
	-Provision of export support
Distribution of information	-Collective action mechanisms (in public-private councils)
	-Use of business chambers
	-Encouragement of firm cooperation/linkages
Improving productivity of forms and entrepreneurs	-Monitoring and assistance for SMEs
	-Infrastructure, funding and management for incubators and cluster formation
	-Promotion of public-private partnerships
	-Upgrading of economic infrastructure

Source: Author's elaboration for Querétaro's case based on the categorisation by Naudé (2010).

want to talk about a Mexican aeronautic industry, there must be Mexican enterprises" (Flores, 2014).

In only ten years, Querétaro was being hailed as a "successful case" of development in regards to its aeronautic sector (Tzitzi & Feix, 2015). Querétaro had grown from having two enterprises to 80 in the sector; forming around 8,000 professionals in the field, while attracting more than 1,500 million dollars in a sector constituted by high-quality employment. Overall, the success of Querétaro's continuity in terms of its economic development policies and, more specifically, Governor Calzada's sectoral policies, was reflected at the end of 2015. For the first time in decades, Querétaro had managed a positive trade balance differential of 200 million dollars. In less than a decade, Querétaro's aeronautic industry had consolidated to the point of contributing 36% of Mexico's exports in that sector. Furthermore, from 2005 to 2014 Querétaro was the Mexican state with the highest annual economic growth average with 5.0% of GDP (Márquez, 2015 based on INEGI, 2016).

Table 5.2 Top five Mexican states regarding annual rate of growth from 2005 to 2014

State	Annual rate of growth
Querétaro	5.0%
Aguascalientes	4.7%
Quintana Roo	4.4%
Zacatecas	4.1%
Nuevo León	4.0%

Source: Author's elaboration based on data from Márquez (2015).

Conclusion

In the new century, the subnational governments' own reconfiguration of developmental policies was essential for them to overcome the industrial challenges that the new globalised context had brought to Mexico. The highest-impact developmental institutions were the formal tripartite "clusters" between government, business and the academy, as well as both formal and informal patterns of state-society relations. Likewise, industrial policies in both Nuevo León and Querétaro were substantially guided by the increasing protagonist role of the SEDESU and the Under-Secretariat of Economic Development, respectively, as the coordinating organisations of industrial policy. In the particular case of Mexico, Nuevo León and Querétaro constitute another testimony of how the subnational level seems to be the better platform for these public-private collaborations in industrial matters – as Schneider (2013, pp. 21–22) has suggested. Furthermore, as in the case of Nuevo León, these public-private collaborations were highly reminiscent of strategies for enhancing industrial transformation in Nordic Europe (Ornston, 2013) and other countries across the globe (Devlin & Moguillansky, 2009).

The circumstances of a new internationalised and more democratic context, however, do keep presenting some formidable challenges. In regards to TNCs, according to economic development officials, the challenge is to positively involve them in their host state's more encompassing goals – creating local suppliers and human capital, enhancing social responsibility and participating jointly in the state's evolving industrial challenges. A more integrated development of Querétaro's local industry, in the case of the aeronautic sector, seems far from over. However, the aforementioned evidence of upgraded local producers presents rewarding results. Furthermore, the creation of more professional and technical human capital has also, thus far, shown some positive effects on the state's living conditions.

It is also worth highlighting the presence of interscalar incompatibility between the policy regimes formulated at the national level (with a neoliberal model) and by the subnational governments of Nuevo León and Querétaro (with a developmental model). Still, in both cases, the success of industrialisation projects did not depend on the subnational level alone as both governments had to devise vertical strategies of integration in order to trigger their jurisdiction's industrialisation. In both cases, vertical strategies of integration looking to finance developmental efforts were shaped by political party affinities. In the case of Nuevo León, the PRI governor relied on the PRI majority in the national congress and the CONAGO organisation of PRI and PRD governors, which resulted in a fiscal decentralisation without precedents in Mexico. In the case of Querétaro, the first step towards building a comparative advantage in the aeronautic sector also relied on party affinity, in that a PAN governor exploited the arrival of the first ever PAN president to get financial support for building Querétaro's new airport and landing the coveted Bombardier investment.

In parallel, both subnational governments formulated a set of continuous industrial policies which were gradually institutionalised in their respective states with an emphasis on state-society developmental coalitions. In the following chapter, the book will redirect the insights gathered from the Mexican case into a comparatist realm. How have other subnational projects of developmentalism been formulated in Latin America and beyond? Can the same elements present in the Mexican cases (e.g. interscalar dynamics and vertical-horizontal strategies) be extrapolated to other countries? Through the following chapters I will argue that the developmental underpinnings extracted from these empirical chapters can very well contribute in analysing other multileveled cases of developmentalism across the globe.

References

Álvarez, E. (2007, November 21). Licitan en diciembre Universidad Aeronáutica. *El Corregidor*.

Becerril, A., & Chávez, M. (2003, July 03). Promueve el Ejecutivo en Querétaro logros panistas. *La Jornada*. [Online]. Retrieved September 14, 2016, from www. jornada.unam.mx/2003/07/03/007n2pol.php?origen=politica.php&fly=

Bennett, D., & Sharpe, K. (1986). Agenda setting and bargaining power: The Mexican State versus transnational automobile corporations. In *The state and development in the third world* (pp. 209–241). Princeton, NJ: Princeton University Press.

Byung, K. (1987). *Bringing and managing socioeconomic change: The state in Korea and Mexico*. Cambridge, MA: Harvard University Press.

Carrillo, M. A., & Salinas, R. J. (2010). Siglo XXI. Sectores industriales emergentes en Querétaro. In *La ciencia, el desarrollo tecnológico y la innovación en Querétaro*. Querétaro: Consejo de Ciencia y Tecnología de Querétaro.

Crónica (2003). Será Aeropuerto de Querétaro "buen regalo" para Fox: gobernador. *Crónica*. [Online]. Retrieved September 14, 2016, from www.cronica.com.mx/notas/2003/59536.html

Daville-Landero, S. (2012). La evolución de la industria de autopartes en Querétaro, 1993–2008. *Economía, Sociedad y Territorio, XII*(40).

Devlin, R., & Moguillansky, G. (2009). Alianzas público-privadas como estrategias nacionales de desarrollo a largo plazo. *Revista Cepal, 97*, 97–116.

Díaz, C. (2014, September 14). Los intentos fallidos de un nuevo aeropuerto para el DF. *Milenio Diario*.

Erfani, J. A. (1995). *The paradox of the Mexican state: Rereading sovereignty from independence to NAFTA*. Boulder, CO: Riener.

Evans, P. (1995). *Embedded autonomy: States and industrial transformation*. Princeton, NJ: Princeton University Press.

Flores, F. (2014, February 12). Despega la industria aeronáutica en Querétaro. *El Financiero*.

Gobierno del Estado de Querétaro (Gobierno Querétaro) (2010). Plan Querétaro 2010–2015. Querétaro: Gobierno del Estado de Querétaro.

Gobierno del Estado de Querétaro (Gobierno Querétaro) (2014). Quinto Informe de Gobierno del Estado de Querétaro. Querétaro: Gobierno del Estado de Querétaro.

González, C. I., & Osorio, L. E. (2000). *Cien años de industria en Querétaro*. Querétaro: Universidad Autónoma de Querétaro.

INEGI (1986). *Estructura económica del estado de Querétaro*. Mexico: Institution Nacional de Estadística y Geografía.

Instituto Nacional de Estadística y Geografía (INEGI) (2016). Cuentas nacionales. www.inegi.org.mx/est/contenidos/proyectos/cn/.México

Johnson, K. (1998). Business-government relations in Mexico since 1990: NAFTA, economic crisis, and the reorganization of business interests. In R. Roett (Ed.), *Mexico's private sector: Recent history, future challenges*. Boulder, CO: Lynne Rienner Publishers.

Márquez, D. (2015, November 2). Reporte económico de entidades. *La Jornada*. Retrieved January 10, 2019 from www.jornada.com.mx/2015/11/02/opinion/022o1eco#

Miranda, E. (2005). *Del Querétaro rural al Querétaro industrial: 1940–1973*. Mexico: Editorial Porrúa.

Molinari, C. (2004). President Fox inaugurates Querétaro Airport. *Business Insight Americas*.

Moreno-Brid, J. C., Santamaría, J., & Valdivia, J. C. R. (2005). Industrialization and economic growth in Mexico after NAFTA: The road travelled. *Development and Change, 36*(6), 1095–1119.

Naudé, W. (2010). *Industrial policy: Old and new issues (No. 2010, 106)*. Working paper//World Institute for Development Economics Research.

Organisation for Economic Co-operation and Development (OECD) (2009). Reviews of Regional Innovation: 15 Mexican States. OECD.

Ornston, D. (2013). Creative corporatism: The politics of high-technology competition in Nordic Europe. *Comparative Political Studies, 46*(6), 702–729.

Schneider, B. R. (2013). *Institutions for effective business-government collaboration: Micro mechanisms and macro politics in Latin America.* Inter-American Developing Bank Working Papers.

Secretaría de Economía (2012). *Industria Aeronáutica en México.* México: Gobierno Federal.

Secretaría de Desarrollo Sustentable del Gobierno Estatal de Querétaro (SEDESU) (2005). *Anuario Económico de Querétaro.* Querétaro: Secretaría de Desarrollo Sustentable de Querétaro.

SEDESU (2010). *Anuario Económico de Querétaro.* Querétaro: Secretaría de Desarrollo Sustentable de Querétaro.

Torres, J. M. (2015, Abril 24). Querétaro se consolida como principal destino de inversión aeroespacial. *Monitor Económico.*

Tzitzi, M., & Feix, N. (2015). Cómo entender el despegue de Querétaro. *Factor Trabajo.* Banco Interamericano de Desarrollo (BID).

6 Subnational industrialisation strategies in Latin America and beyond

Introduction

After exploring the developmental strategies and policies that were woven from below by two subnational governments in Mexico, this chapter will look to explore strategies, patterns and factors that may enrich a comparative assessment across subnational governments from other countries. In this order of ideas, the present chapter seeks to extrapolate Mexico's experiences to two other developing countries, Brazil and India, in an effort to underscore how, amid differentiated economic and democratic transitions, subnational units of government deployed multileveled strategies of industrialisation to trigger their jurisdictions' economic development.

The guiding questions remain the same: What were the strategies that contributed to achieving an industrial transformation across these varying countries? And how did multilevel characteristics affect these strategies within countries that are so vastly populated and territorially extensive? In order to explore possible answers to these questions, I have considered two subnational case studies, from Brazil and India, which have already been covered to varying degree in the developmental literature with distinct traits and themes: Minas Gerais, in the case of Brazil, and Gujarat, in the case of India.

After reviewing these two case studies, I will also undertake a brief overview of "failed" or "negative cases" of subnational developmental strategies. In the words of Landman (2003), the objective of assessing negative cases is to highlight or "include instances in which the outcome of interest does not occur" (p. 77). In this study, the "outcome of interest" is the achievement of an industrial transformation at the subnational level. Therefore, this section on negative cases will make an effort to diagnose what variables or factors were either missing or deficient, and which generated as a consequence a failed implementation of a developmental strategy at the subnational level. To assess these failed strategies I will refer briefly to subnational testimonies from Mexico, India, Brazil and Peru as "failed" or "negative cases" of policy transformation from below, with the aim of highlighting the comparative implications that this research could have for the developmental literature.

Toward a comparative assessment of multilevel developmentalism in Brazil and India

As mentioned briefly in the first chapter, the industrial trajectories of Mexico and Brazil have long been assessed side by side considering the affinity of the industrialisation strategies (and industrial "miracles") that they both formulated during the mid-20th century. Ben Ross Schneider (1999) paired these "desarrollista states", due to the recurrent tendencies of cronyism and fragmentation, as divergent and deficient cases of the developmental states that were so successful in East Asia. Still, these Latin American States managed to "stretch" (Evans, 1995) their organisational capacities in order to achieve impressive rates of growth, landing in a sort of limbo between being a "predatory" and a "developmental" state, which Peter Evans defined appropriately as an "intermediate state". In this same comparative assessment, however, Evans strayed away from the traditional pairing of Brazil with Mexico by pairing Brazil with India instead. In the words of Evans (1995), "neither Brazil nor India could generate the public-private symbiosis that was the key to Korea's success" (p. 149), nor could they construct the "institutional framework" (p. 152) necessary to achieve a full-fledged developmental success.

Eventually, this inclusion of India along with Brazil and Mexico by reason of their developmental trajectories was further echoed by Atul Kohli (2004). Kohli, however, places greater emphasis on State power than on the public-private collaboration and bureaucratic professionalism emphasised by Evans' embedded autonomy. Through this approach to Brazil's and India's State consolidation, Kohli reaches a comparative typology which echoes the preceding arguments on state fragmentation and multilevel characteristics.

On the one side, Korea is described as "cohesive-capitalist" with authoritarian characteristics, extensive penetration or surveillance of its society, links with big business groups, a competent bureaucracy and tight control of labour – characteristics which were firmly exploited to achieve rapid industrialisation. On the other side, Brazil and India are classified as "fragmented-multiclass states", where political and social cleavages impeded a more cohesive drive towards national development in the long term.

Thus, when fragmented-multiclass states such as Brazil and India wanted to mobilise economic and human resources towards industrialisation, Kohli argues (2004), "tax-collecting capacities were limited, public-spending priorities included numerous goals other than growth promotion, attempts to direct credit easily evolved into cronyism", and any potential failure in these industrialising attempts was considered a risk by political elites as it could, in turn, jeopardise their political careers (p. 14).

Although the aforementioned accounts of industrialisation have proven to be illuminating around themes of state-society relations and State capacity when it comes to triggering a country's industrialisation, there is still an untold story of how subnational platforms interact, adapt and contribute to national policies of developmentalism. Kohli (2004) does manage to enlighten this fact by acknowledging the historical importance that the "politics of governors" has had in Brazil's history. Much could be obtained, therefore, if there is a more multileveled assessment of these countries' development, shedding the traditional approaches which consider the nation-State as the sole level of analysis.

In the words of the Indian scholar Aseema Sinha (2005), "limiting analytical attention to the top-down centralized state blinds us to the crucial regional responses to that state", responses which, moreover, "prove to be directly consequential for investment flows and institutional changes in many countries" (p. 4). Consequently, a multilevel approximation to development can elucidate how centre-periphery dynamics are essential in attaining the developmental outcomes initially pursued.

The following sections will thus continue to build on the multilevel framework of analysis to assess the two-tiered strategies that were pursued by subnational governments in Brazil and India in order to achieve an industrial transformation.

Minas Gerais amid Brazilian *Desenvolvimentismo*

Brazil's political history from the end of the 19th up until the end of the 20th century evolved across a continuum of not so democratic regimes, authoritarian regimes and, finally, democratic regimes. First, from 1889 to 1930, Brazil's "Old" or "First Republic" was dominated by regional oligarchs and an alliance between two of the wealthier states in Brazil: São Paulo and Minas Gerais, which arranged the selection of Brazil's president for years in what was eventually termed the political pact of "coffee with milk", based on the economic strongholds of São Paulo (coffee industry) and Minas Gerais (dairy industry).

Afterwards, Getulio Vargas and his Estado Novo initiated a centralising effort by Brazil's governmental authorities, though this eventually gave way to regional pacts among governors to demobilise political and social unrest. Nonetheless, Brazil's "Second Republic" broke through from 1946 to 1964, implementing democratic elections which "proved to be among the freest in Brazil's history" (Skidmore, Smith & Green, 2010, p. 330). Succeeding political crises, however, gave way to yet another authoritarian regime consisting of military rule which would finally stage a gradual re-democratisation of the country's political system throughout the 1980s.

Inflation, economic crises and the boom-and bust cycles of its economy, led by its reliance on commodity sectors, had a reiterative presence throughout these varying political stages of Brazil's history, with its Industrial Miracle (1930–1970) representing an eventual breather in the economic turbulence. Throughout these stages, however, the Brazilian state of Minas Gerais has been frequently brought up in the country's analysis as an example of a state with positive industrial outcomes and institutions (see Montero, 2002; Eaton, 2004).

How has this state managed to, first, consolidate its industry and, then, reposition it amid intermittent economic crises? And what has been the role of its subnational government in this outcome? After assessing the existing literature on Brazil's and Minas Gerais' development, I detected subnational strategies, both vertical and horizontal, that echo the findings of the research undertaken among Mexico's subnational states. In a similar tone, therefore, the following section will detail those shared patterns of developmental strategies that resonate with subnational industrialisation strategies beyond Minas Gerais.

Strategies of vertical integration in Minas Gerais

As a starting point, then, Minas Gerais' strategies to integrate their economic development priorities into a national platform should be highlighted. This is, again, where issues of federalism and intergovernmental relations come into play. Moreover, it is worth noting that the timing with which intergovernmental relations take place can also trigger path-dependent mechanisms that shape both subnational and national platforms in the long run. As highlighted by Eaton (2004), during the end of the 19th century Latin American States did not have as much political or organisational capacity as they had during the mid-20th century. This weakness of the State's centre in the region therefore expanded the opportunities of local elites (the so-called *caudillos* in Latin America) to oppose the national government and assert their will on political and economic matters.

In the case of Brazil, it was the governors who amassed the largest power below the centre, and, furthermore, it was the governors of the stronger provinces who thus represented the major opposition to the central government. It is worth stressing that, as exemplified by the "coffee with milk" politics, Minas Gerais traditionally had a strong position in Brazil's political and economic development. Accordingly, when it came to devising the distribution of economic resources and tax revenues during the First Republic, São Paulo and Minas Gerais had a larger say, to the detriment of the national government's authorities and also weaker provinces or states.

The latter was ultimately reflected in Brazil's Constitution of 1891, which "allowed states to set their own taxes on exports, borrow revenues abroad, design their own constitutions, and maintain separate military forces and electoral and judicial codes" (Eaton, 2004, p. 76; see also Campello de Souza, 1968). During the First Republic, the decentralisation of fiscal resources and authorities thus strengthened the position of Minas Gerais within Brazil by allowing the subnational government to collect taxes on the export of its commodities. Nonetheless, the surmountable challenge that Minas Gerais soon had to face was transitioning from an agricultural to an industrial economy – following the industrialising prerogatives that were established with Vargas' Estado Novo in Brazil and with the structuralism of the Economic Commission for Latin America and the Caribbean (ECLAC) across the Latin American region a few decades later.

Despite Getulio Vargas' recentralisation strategies, the political leaders of Minas Gerais again managed to integrate their interests with Vargas' industrialising project through their committed political support. As a reward, Minas Gerais obtained access to the industrial policy priorities of the Estado Novo and landed important industrial projects in the mining sector (Montero, 2002, p. 63). After the Estado Novo ended, political elites deployed the same strategies of political support in exchange for public investments, which eventually reshaped the state's industrial outlook by providing it with the developmental Centrais Elétricas de Minas Gerais (CEMIG) and the steel SOEs Usiminas during the Kubitschek presidency (1956–1961), and Acominas once the military regime had seized power in the mid-1960s (Schneider, 1991, p. 124).

The reiterated integration that *mineiro* elites achieved, under either democratic or military regimes, secured them essential economic resources and projects for industries which were deemed as national priorities within the ISI emphasis of Brazil's National Development Plans. These economic resources were also used by *mineiro* governors to finance the creation and consolidation of the state's developmental agencies. "As a result", in the words of Alfred Montero (2002), "much of the stunning growth of state-led industrialization during the 'Brazilian miracle' could be observed within the political boundaries of Minas Gerais" (p. 65).

Besides this agile intergovernmental strategies formulated by Minas Gerais elites there was, furthermore, a direct integration of *mineiro* technocrats and political officials within the developmental agencies of the national government throughout Brazil's several development stages, which secured them a second channel of policy and resource access (see Montero, 2002; Hagopian, 2006; Schneider, 1991). In particular, Schneider (1991) highlights the importance of having multiple *mineiro* officials jumping into key economic positions in the national government, as they formulated a stronger bond between national and subnational policies. This point is also echoed by Montero (2002), when describing how "the circulation of these elites between the state government's planning apparatus and that of the national state provided an additional link between the interests of *mineiro* economic policy and national developmentalist programs" (p. 65).

Eventually, when Brazil's third wave of democratisation took root during the 1980s, the governors would again use their leverage over national legislators to expand the fiscal decentralisation of resources and authorities – mostly to the benefit, once more, of Brazil's most developed states, such as Minas Gerais and São Paulo (Eaton, 2004, pp. 157–158). This fiscal decentralisation included both taxation authority and direct federal transfers to states and municipalities without the traditional ear-marking established by the extinct military regime (Britto, 1998). As a direct result of the fiscal decentralisation of the new Constitution of 1988, Brazilian states' revenues increased from 22% to 26% (Britto, 1998, p. 700). Furthermore, the new constitution also laid the groundwork for states and their developmental banks to print their own money in an unprecedented devolution of economic attributions (see Eaton, 2004, p. 159).

Strategies of horizontal institutionalisation in Minas Gerais

In parallel, throughout the 20th century, Minas Gerais exploited the vast increase in fiscal resources and attributions to expand its own developmental capacities and institutions. The integration of *mineiro* officials within the national government's developmental apparatus was likewise essential in scaling up the developmental priorities of their home state. Now, although Minas Gerais usually had an advantageous political and economic position at the start of the 20th century, by the 1950s their industrial outlook was still severely limited due to a lack of infrastructural capacities – a recurrent theme in developing countries' first industrial transformation (see Hirschman, 1958; Gerschenkron, 1962). Gradually, however, State elites began to share a vision of the state's industrial transformation with the hopes of integrating Minas Gerais into the Brazilian economy. In the words of Ruiz and Andrade (2012), these state political, agrarian, intellectual and industrial elites "recognised the situation of economic backwardness of the state and were able to converge on a strategy of 'recovery of lost time'", which included "precocious" subnational activities of planning and the formation of a technocracy with a developmental mind-set (p. 157).

Subsequent programmes elaborated by the subnational government – the Plano de Recuperação Econômica e Fomento da Produção of 1947 and Plano da Electrifação of 1951 – evidenced the commitment that it had to setting the bases for the state's industrial future. Immediately afterwards, as part of his government slogan "Energia e Transporte", Governor Kubitschek spearheaded in 1952 the creation of the developmental agency CEMIG precisely to remediate the state's lack of electrical infrastructure, along with making substantial investments in the state's road system (Ruiz & Andrade, 2012). Minas Gerais' industrial and infrastructural prospects were further benefitted by Kubitschek's ascension to the presidential chair in 1956.

The gradual progress of Minas Gerais' industrialisation led the state to become an epitome of horizontal institutionalisation in the 1960s, with the creation of key developmental agencies or "an efficient institutional apparatus to support industrialisation" (Ruiz & Andrade, 2012, p. 160), which led the state's definitive industrial transformation: the Development Bank of Minas Gerais (BDMG), Institute of Industrial Development (INDI) and Company of Industrial Districts (CDI). From this point forward, the BDMG would appropriate a sort of pilot agency role for the state's development, which was evidenced in its Diagnóstico da Economia Mineira (Diagnostic of Minas Gerais' Economy) of 1968.

During the 1970s, the institutionalisation of Minas Gerais' industrial policy began to show noteworthy results. In the capital goods sector, its economy expanded from 7.3% in 1970 to 19.8% in 1980; by that same year of 1980, Minas Gerais was producing 20% of the country's capital goods, representing a 12% increase from the year 1970 (Montero, 2002, p. 73). The structure of the *mineiro* economy was redrawn within a decade, emphasising a clear transition towards industry (see Table 6.1).

Minas Gerais' developmental mission seemed well under way, but the economic crises of the 1980s, which were particularly impacting in Latin America, threatened to jeopardise the state's progress. At a national scale, Brazil's democratic transition was accompanied by structural reforms which intended to reduce the State's intervention in the economy. According to Montero (2002), this "dual transition" of democratisation and regime liberalisation

Table 6.1 Evolution of Minas Gerais' GDP distribution by economic sector (1970–1980)

	Agriculture	*Industry*	*Services*
1970	17.9%	25.4%	56.6%
1980	17.7%	38.9%	43.2%

Source: Author's elaboration based on data from Ruiz & Andrade, 2012 (p. 162).

enabled subnational governments to "claim new abilities to implement economic reforms of their own in response to the economic crises central governments seemed incapable of redressing completely" (p. 42).

By the end of the 1990s, nonetheless, BDMG, along with Minas Gerais' subnational government, would again assume the role of pushing for a proactive industrial policy, in contrast to the neoliberal model implemented by President Cardoso at the national level, through an approach based on strategic sectors, internationalisation and public-private collaboration with business associations and automotive multinational companies such as FIAT and Mercedes-Benz. As a consequence, Minas Gerais would continue to consolidate its position as one of Brazil's leading industrial states throughout the start of the new century.

Gujarat amid Indian *dirigisme*

Once an analysis of India is begun, it is pretty clear that at a national or aggregate level this nation-State presents likewise some of the familiar challenges for Latin American States: social and political cleavages, a vast territory and population and, up until the end of the 20th century, a rather unfulfilled promise of their development potential. India, too, as in the cases of Mexico and Brazil, has had an ambiguous assessment of its development. As shown by Evans (1995) and Kohli (2004), it can well be considered as an intermediate State, between a developmental failure and a developmental success, or, at least, as a State that has at times attained rewarding outcomes regarding its economic development.

Quite similar to Latin American States, India was expected to share the developmental success of the East Asian Tigers. Its potential since independence was, however, greater as it already had one of the key ingredients that the East Asian Tigers forged in their developmental path and that the Latin American States had historically lacked: a meritocratic bureaucracy.

Immediately after its independence in 1947, India implemented planned industrialisation as the main economic model to overcome economic backwardness, following a global trend that was already taking shape in the developing world. It implemented protectionism across the majority of economic sectors, invested highly in infrastructural upgrading and financed domestic entrepreneurs' ventures through the creation of development banks (Chandrasekhar, 2010). Furthermore, in efforts to centralise and control the country's development, the national government recurred to the "licence-raj" system: "a system of industrial licensing that regulated and restricted entry of new firms and expansion of existing ones" established in the country's 1951 Industries Development and Regulation Act (Aghion, Burgess, Redding, & Zilibotti, 2008, p. 2).

During the first decade of India's *dirigisme*, as its planned industrialisation model was named, the country managed to achieve high rates of growth, averaging 7.2% from 1950 until the mid-1960s, comparable to those of East Asia's Tigers (Chandrasekhar, 2010, p. 32). By the 1970s, however, it was widely acknowledged that the licensing system had not been effective in triggering rapid industrialisation – and it would continue to be ineffective for the following decades. From 1960 to 1990, India grew at an average of 3.5% per year.

In the 1990s, nonetheless, India's development story began to change, as it grew at an average of 6% per year coupled with the regime's economic liberalisation. This change of economic fate led scholars to the familiar assessment of State- vs market-oriented models. Given that India implemented a State-interventionist model from the 1960s until the end of the 1980s through its "licence-raj" or regulatory system, analysts have considered it as a State failure; on the other hand, given that the increased growth rates occurred after India's economic liberalisation, analysts have given the credit for this to the markets. Therefore, in the words of Sinha (2005), "the Indian model of development seemed to confirm that state failure was more crippling than market failures" (p. 7).

Below the national level, however, there was evidence that India's regional variation had given way to states or provinces achieving developmental outcomes both before and after India's liberalisation. The question, then, is what led some subnational governments (such as Gujarat) to have better results in their development when compared to other Indian states which had the same or more developmental potential? When I assessed Sinha's (2005) study of India's regionally divergent development, I found it echoed the multilevel or two-tiered strategies that I had detected in both Mexican and Brazilian subnational units. The following sections will thus highlight the vertical and horizontal strategies that were deployed by Gujarat's government to achieve its developmental trajectory.

Strategies of vertical integration in Gujarat

One of the recurrent traits that fragmented States have, besides social and political cleavages, is a disparity between their regions, provinces or states. As a consequence, this galvanised reconfiguration at the subnational level has historically posited challenges to the uniformity of those States. These problems have been accentuated in India by it being the most populous democracy of the world and having one of the vastest territories in Asia. And it is in this regional diversity and lack of centralisation that subnational governments, such as Gujarat, have tried to appropriate attributions and resources in order to trigger their development.

Gujarat is a state in northwest India. At the time of India's independence in 1947, it consisted of one of the country's largest princely states (the Baroda state), 395 other princely states and a territorial unit with several districts under British rule (Ahmedabad, Kheda, Panchmahals, Bharouch and the Surat district of the Bombay presidency) (Sinha, 2005, p. 180).

In 1960, the national government separated the former Bombay state from Gujarat, which resulted eventually in two states: Gujarat and Maharashtra. The partition of Gujarat took away one of its most developed units in Bombay, threatening the state's economic future. Eventually, having the thriving economy of Bombay within a neighbouring state would form a sort of developmental consensus among Gujarat's political and entrepreneurial elites, leading them to put emphasis on the necessity of transitioning from an agricultural to an industrial economy.

The industrialisation of Gujarat was nonetheless substantially constrained by the centralised planning that India's federal government was pursuing at the time (Dholakia, 2000; Hirway, Kashyap & Shah, 2002). The 1951 Industries Development and Regulation Act intended to secure the national government's control over the country's industrialisation. According to Aghion et al. (2008), industrial licences, which were issued by a Licensing Committee of the Ministry of Industrial Development, were required for the following: (i) establishment of a new factory, (ii) continuation of activities in a factory without an industrial licence, (iii) substantial expansion of the capacity of an existing factory, (iv) introduction of a new process or product or (v) modification of the factory's location.

Besides the "licence-raj" system, the federal government had a strongly centralised command of the country's financial resources. Due to its high levels of political centralisation prior to the liberalising reforms, India was even considered a "quasi-federal" system, whose centralisation was intensified by the predominance of its public sector in industry, along with the federal government's allocation of resources (Rao, 2003, p. 32). The centralised attributions of the federal government, along with the ongoing role of its Planning Commission and Finance Commission, made the Indian states traditionally dependent on the centre – a feature that would survive into the new century (Singh, 2004). As a result, during Indian *dirigisme*, it was the federal government's discretionary criteria that decided *which* industrial projects were viable, *which* industrial projects merited public investment and *where* they could be located through the emission of industrial licences.

To overcome these discretionary constraints established by the federal government, Gujarat's political elites developed vertical strategies of integration with the national government or what Sinha (2005, pp. 92–93) called "bureaucratic infiltration": this consisted of Gujarat Industry Department officials' establishment of both formal and informal contacts with officials from the federal Ministry of Industry to acquire support regarding industrial projects and industrial licences, and information on the national government's industrial priorities.

In the words of Sinha (2005), "Gujarat's strategy was to work slowly but persistently at building channels of political access inside the bureaucracy", meaning that Gujarat's "officials were in constant touch with various layers of the industrial bureaucracy in New Delhi" (p. 97). Consequently, not only were Gujarat's officials able to accommodate their industrial projects to the priorities of the national government, but they also secured approval for a majority of the industrial licences that were applied for either to start or to expand industries within Gujarat.

By the year 1980, Gujarat was already ranked in fourth place among Indian states based on its contribution to the country's manufacturing sector; a decade later, by the year 1990, they would end up surpassing every other Indian state in this field (Awasthi, 2002, p. 167). In the words of Awasthi (2002), Gujarat "achieved this spectacular success because of its entrepreneurial endowment, progressive policies and political will of the government. . ., proactive and efficient bureaucracy, conducive industrial relations" and the continuing consolidation of its infrastructural and industrial capacities (p. 166). The following section will thus highlight the horizontal strategies that were deployed by Gujarat in pursuit of its industrial transformation, including elements cited by Awasthi, such as its "progressive policies" and its "conducive industrial relations" between government and entrepreneurs.

Strategies of horizontal institutionalisation in Gujarat

As evidenced by prior analyses of subnational strategies, vertical strategies have enabled subnational governments to access economic resources and to be part of developmental priorities held by the national government. In parallel to achieving this vertical integration between centre and periphery, it is of equal importance for subnational governments to construct favourable developmental institutions in their jurisdictions. In the industrial transformation of Gujarat, this tandem of vertical and horizontal strategies was also fundamental to insert the state into India's industrialising path.

Either through the already classical lens of "embedded autonomy" (Evans, 1995) regarding state-capital relations or through the more recent emphasis on establishing the "correct institutions" (Hausmann, Rodrik, & Sabel, 2008), an institutionalisation of industrial strategies has generally been a cornerstone for successful instances of rapid industrialisation. In the institutionalist literature of developmental studies, furthermore, the meritocracy of the State's bureaucracy has also been highlighted as a key variable for developmental success (Evans, 1995; Johnson, 1982). It is then in this particular variable (bureaucracy) that India has a considerable advantage over Mexico and Brazil, where there is a lack of meritocracy and a higher persistence of patronage dynamics.

In the case of Gujarat, on the horizontal axis of analysis, the continuous institutionalisation of industrial strategies coupled with its meritocratic bureaucracy enabled it to supersede other Indian states which seemed to have much more potential to consolidate their industrial development since independence. And its policy transformation is better attested in the creation of subnational or regional institutions, which led the state's industrial strategies.

Sinha's (2005) assessment of regional variation in India's development highlights how three Indian states (Gujarat, Tamil Nadu and West Bengal) deployed similar industrial incentives to trigger their region's development prior to India's liberalisation: tax incentives, subsidies, finance and industrial estates, among others; however, it was Gujarat's more formal and continuous institutionalisation of its industrial policies that gave it a comparative edge when fostering industrial projects in the state, which is reflected in the creation and coordination of agency mechanisms such as its Gujarat Export Corporation, iNDEXTb and its Licensing Monitoring Cell.

In the words of Sinha (2005), "the existence of a specialized agency in Gujarat – iNDEXTb – that was responsible for making the information regarding the state's industrial policies available to all investors facilitated the implementation of various incentives" (p. 140), whereas in Tamil Nadu, "no specialized agency existed to make that information on policies available in a coherent form" (p. 141), thus leading to lower investments in Tamil Nadu.

These analyses undertaken by Sinha portray how Gujarat outpaced two other leading provinces, West Bengal and Tamil Nadu, through a continuous set of industrial policies focused on promoting investment both from the private sector and from the central government, while empowering a ministry of industry (the Gujarat Industrial Investment Corporation) as a sort of pilot agency for the region's economic development. The contrast of strategies between these three provinces eventually generated a substantial difference in industrial indicators such as investment rates, growth and regulation efficiency.

Table 6.2 Creation of subnational industrial agencies in Gujarat

Agency	Objective	Year of creation
Gujarat Export Corporation Ltd.	Export promotion	1965
Licensing Monitoring Cell	Supervision of industrial licence applications	1969
Industrial Extension Bureau (iNDEXTb)	Investment promotion	1977

Source: Author's elaboration.

Negative cases of subnational industrialisation in Latin America and beyond

The principal aim of my application of the "method of agreement" to Mexico's subnational cases of industrialisation, and the subsequent extrapolation of the findings to Minas Gerais and Gujarat, is to highlight what I consider to be the main factors or "independent variables": the presence of both vertical integration and horizontal institutionalisation strategies conducted by subnational governments. As a result of the conjuncture of these multileveled strategies, an industrial transformation crystallised in these subnational states – whilst emphasising as well the importance of institutions regarding economic development (see Acemoglu & Robinson, 2012; Hausmann et al., 2008).

However, I am not pretending to state that vertical integration between subnational and national governments and horizontal institutionalisation are sufficient to achieve an industrial transformation, because other variables matter as well. In the case of Mexico, it seems farfetched to think of a structural transformation in southern states such as Chiapas or Guerrero, considering Mexico's regional disparities, or what Dávila, Kessel, and Levy (2002) call a "distortion of comparative advantages" that has inhibited the southeast throughout Mexico's development.

Rather, what this book acknowledges from the start is that, in the words of De Schweinitz (1964, p. 7), these independent variables were "necessary but not sufficient conditions". The dependent variable for my case studies was thus an industrial transformation evidenced either in the construction of a comparative industrial advantage or in the transition to higher technological sectors as a response to national and international challenges.

Likewise, I do not intend to say that geography or the timing of the cases' industrial transformation did not matter. Rather, one of my arguments is that subnational governments that managed to access federal resources and/or developmental priorities at a national level and, at the same time, formulated a continuous set of industrial policies with an emphasis on public-private collaboration were better positioned to exploit a favourable constellation of factors – be it geography, timing, national industrialisation momentum, state-society synergies or foreign or domestic capital, to name a few.

This assessment can be better put into perspective by contrasting it with the results of "negative cases": subnational states which shared similar potential or conditions for achieving a successful developmental policy regime but failed due to an absence of either the vertical or the horizontal axis of strategies evaluated thus far. After a review of the growing literature on subnational strategies of industrialisation, I was able to detect subnational cases in which the "expected result" or the dependent variable varied in a negative undertone.

In the case of Brazil, Montero's (2002) study of the developmental shortfalls of Rio de Janeiro evidences how the continuous exploitation of economic resources within clientelistic strategies hampered the necessary institutionalisation of industrial policies that could have led the state to the developmental outcomes achieved by Minas Gerais. The persistence of patronage or *cacicazgo* (local strongmen) politics in Latin America continues to constrain the developmental potential of subnational units – a case that has resonated throughout the past decades in Mexico, as reflected in the northern state Coahuila (Freidenberg, 2017) or the central state Estado de Mexico (Nichter & Palmer-Rubin, 2014). As has been underscored by Montero, a state's development priorities are usually jeopardised when the governor's concerns are primarily related to his/her political career.

Accordingly, this "politicisation" of development in Rio de Janeiro, for instance, led not to the disappearance of industrial policies, but to the formulation of industrial policies pursuing the consolidation of "the clientelistic base of their political benefactors", in which political elites "exerted direct control over developmental organizations" (Montero, 2002, pp. 144–145). The overall result of Rio de Janeiro's politicisation of its development has been reflected, among other issues, in its marked loss of competitiveness as a regional economy within Brazil (Azzoni, 2017). Instead of exploiting the financial resources that were decentralised during both protectionist and open market phases of Brazil (see Eaton, 2004) for developmental objectives, Rio de Janeiro distributed them to strengthen pre-existing clientelistic schemes. Rio de Janeiro consequently represents a marked deficiency in the developmental construction of its horizontal institutions.

In regards to the absence of vertical integration between centre and periphery, two subnational cases come in mind. In the case of India's regionalised development, Sinha (2005) has highlighted how the strategies of confrontation elaborated by West Bengal towards the centre during both the pre- and post-liberalisation periods constrained its economic development by generating lower percentages of public investment and approved industrial licences. As a result of these conflictual relationships with the centre, Sinha defines West Bengal as an "isolationist non-productive state", as opposed to Gujarat being a "vertically integrated developmental state" with higher rates of investment (Sinha, 2003, p. 467).

Quite similar to this analysis of vertical confrontation leading to a developmental shortfall is Eaton's (2017) portrayal of Peru's "subnational policy challenge" in various regions. According to Eaton (2017), "the maintenance of a profoundly neoliberal national policy regime since 1990 has triggered efforts by a variety of left-of-center regional presidents to deviate from neoliberalism" (p. 51); the lack of subnational capacities, however, has thus far impeded regional or subnational governments from consolidating a successful policy regime from below. This resonates with the main predicament that this book has formulated: the need that subnational governments have of formulating an industrial strategy not only within their jurisdiction, but also *above* their jurisdiction given the attributions that are exclusive to federal or central governments.

Conclusion

Although in the past decades States have gone through an organisational reconfiguration which has devolved considerable attributions to the intermediate and lower levels of governments, it is evident that subnational strategies are always contingent on the national context. Even in an increasingly globalised and decentralised world, the nation-State still has a monopoly over particular economic resources and policy domains. As a consequence, subnational agency will continue to be structurally constrained or bound by national governments. Still, the "policy space" that is available for subnational governments since the third wave of democratisation seems to be unprecedented and thus merits more case-by-case analyses to assess both developmental successes and failures.

Regarding the current chapter's comparative outlook, my research on Mexico has seemingly found an echo in analytical explorations of other developing countries, particularly when considering Sinha's (2005) contemplation of both "horizontal" and "vertical interactions" across government levels. The main finding presented by Sinha regarding Gujarat's success, which echoes the subnational strategies highlighted in Mexico and Brazil, is that the provincial government's strategies were necessarily twofold: firstly, a vertical interaction with the centre with the objective of attracting major investments and opportunities within the national industrial priorities, and secondly, a horizontal strategy based on the continuous institutionalisation of its industrial policy.

Montero's (2002) approximation to subnational industrialisation strategies is similar when one considers "delegative government" and "horizontal embeddedness" as causal factors for Minas Gerais' and Asturias' developmental success. Montero's independent variables (delegative government and horizontal embeddedness) are, however, more constrained to the subnational level. His assessment of "delegative government" is characterised by subnational or regional leaders who choose to delegate developmental attributions and resources to their states' agencies based on the socio-political context of their state. These variables eventually leave out the strategies of vertical integration that I highlighted between national and subnational governments – e.g. fiscal decentralisation, policy access, and collaboration between developmental elites and agencies, among others – although

Montero does consider these interactions in detail, as has been the case with other seminal works on Minas Gerais' development (Schneider, 1991; Hagopian, 1994; Eaton, 2004).

The aim of this chapter, therefore, was to extrapolate the independent variables that had been analysed in the Mexican case studies to underscore their salience within other cases of subnational industrialisation. Accordingly, it has shown how despite cross-national and cross-subnational differences, these subnational case studies "agreed" or relied on very similar multileveled strategies in their path towards industrialisation.

References

Acemoglu, D., & Robinson, J. A. (2012). *Why nations fail: The origins of power, prosperity, and poverty*. New York, NY: Crown Publishers.

Aghion, P., Burgess, R., Redding, S. J., & Zilibotti, F. (2008). The unequal effects of liberalization: Evidence from dismantling the License Raj in India. *American Economic Review*, *98*(4), 1397–1412.

Awasthi, D. N. (2002). Recent changes in industrial economy of Gujarat. Issues and evidences. In I. Hirway, S. P. Kashyap, & A. Shah (Eds.), *Dynamics of development in Gujarat*. New Delhi: Concept Publishing Company.

Azzoni, C. R. (2017). Recent trends in regional competitiveness and industrial concentration. In *Revival: Structure and Structural Change in the Brazilian Economy*. Abingdon: Routledge Press.

Britto, R. (1998). La Federación en Brasil: Impasses y Perspectivas. In C. Alba, I. Bizberg, & R. H. Ilán (Eds.), *Las regiones ante la globalización*. México: El Colegio de México.

Campello de Souza, M. D. C. (1968). O processo político-partidário na Primeira República. In *Brasil em perspectiva*, *20*, 162–226.

Chandrasekhar, C. (2010). From dirigisme to neoliberalism: Aspects of the political economy of the transition in India. *Development and Society*, *39*(1), 29–59.

Dávila, E., Kessel, G., & Levy, S. (2002). El sur también existe: un ensayo sobre el desarrollo regional de México. *Economía Mexicana*, *XI*, pp. 203–207.

De Schweinitz, K. (1964). *Industrialization and democracy*. Illinois: Free Press of Glencoe.

Dholakia, R. H. (2000). Liberalisation in Gujarat: Review of recent experience. *Economic and Political Weekly*, 3121–3124.

Eaton, K. (2004). *Politics beyond the capital: The design of subnational institutions in South America*. Stanford, CA: Stanford University Press.

Eaton, K. (2017). Policy regime juxtaposition in Latin America. *Colombia Internacional*, (90), 37–65.

Evans, P. (1995). *Embedded autonomy: States and industrial transformation*. Princeton, NJ: Princeton University Press.

Freidenberg, F. (2017). La otra representación: vínculos clientelares a nivel local en México. *Andamios*, *14*(34), 231–258.

Gerschenkron, A. (1962). *Economic backwardness in historical perspective*. Cambridge, MA: Belknap Press of Harvard University Press.

Hagopian, F. (1994). *Traditional politics against state transformation in Brazil*. In Migdal, J., Kohli, A. & Shue, V. (Eds.) State power and social forces: Domination and transformation in the third world. Cambridge: Cambridge University Press.

Hagopian, F. (2006). *Traditional politics and regime change in Brazil*. Cambridge: Cambridge University Press.

Hausmann, R., Rodrik, D., & Sabel, C. (2008). *Reconfiguring industrial policy: A framework with an application to South Africa*. Working paper. Cambridge, MA: John F. Kennedy School of Government.

Hirschman, A. O. (1958). *The strategy of economic development*. New Haven, CT: Yale University Press.

Hirway, I., Kashyap, S. P., & Shah, A. (Eds.). (2002). *Dynamics of development in Gujarat*. New Delhi: Concept Publishing Company.

Johnson, C. (1982). *MITI and the Japanese miracle: The growth of industrial policy: 1925–1975*. Stanford, CA: Stanford University Press.

Kohli, A. (2004). *State-directed development: Political power and industrialization in the global periphery*. Cambridge: Cambridge University Press.

Landman, T. (2003). *Issues and methods in comparative politics: An introduction*. Abingdon: Routledge.

Montero, A. P. (2002). *Shifting states in global markets: Subnational industrial policy in contemporary Brazil and Spain*. University Park, PA: Penn State University Press.

Nichter, S., & Palmer-Rubin, B. (2014). Clientelism, declared support and Mexico's 2012 campaign. In J. I. Domínguez, K. F. Greene, C. H. Lawson, & A. Moreno (Eds.), *Mexico's evolving democracy: A comparative study of the 2012 elections* (pp. 200–226). Baltimore, MD: John Hopkins University Press.

Rao, M. G. (2003). Fiscal decentralization in China and India: A comparative perspective. *Asia Pacific Development Journal, 10*(1), 25–46.

Ruiz, J., & Andrade, D. C. (2012). Panorama geral da industrialização de Minas Gerais (1970–2000). *Leituras de Economia Política, 9*(12).

Schneider, B. R. (1991). *Politics within the state: Elite bureaucrats and industrial policy in authoritarian Brazil*. Pittsburgh, PA: University of Pittsburgh Press.

Schneider, B. R. (1999). The Desarrollista state in Brazil and Mexico. In M. Woo-Cummings (Ed.), *The developmental state* (pp. 276–305). Ithaca, NY: Cornell University Press.

Singh, N. (2004). *India's System of Intergovernmental Fiscal Relations (No. 578)*. Working Papers, UC Santa Cruz Economics Department.

Sinha, A. (2003). Rethinking the developmental state model: Divided leviathan and subnational comparisons in India. *Comparative Politics*, 459–476.

Sinha, A. (2005). *The regional roots of developmental politics in India: A divided leviathan*. Indiana: Indiana University Press.

Skidmore, T. E., Smith, P. H., & Green, J. N. (2010). *Modern Latin America*. New York, NY: Oxford University Press.

7 Conclusion
Transforming industrial policy from below

Introduction

By shifting the focus from nation-States to subnational governments, this analysis has made an effort to study the responses and intergovernmental dynamics that are inherent to multileveled and regionally divergent States such as Mexico. With the comparative assessment explored in chapter 6, furthermore, this work hopes to build upon an emerging field of studies focused on the development strategies devised by subnational governments before and after the multilevel conjuncture emphasised throughout the book – meaning the constellation of democratisation, decentralisation and globalisation movements.

This concluding section will therefore return to the central questions put forward since the initial chapter: How can we assess subnational industrialisation efforts within the developing world? And what have been the implications of the ongoing State reconfigurations for developmental efforts? Overall, this chapter will summarize the findings and insights provided by the case studies in an effort to distil the main variables or factors that have been present in industrial transformations led by subnational governments.

As a departing point, it seems rather clear that these subnational testimonies are, in fact, transferrable among developing contexts. Due to the structural constraints that a federal system imposes on intermediate levels of government, there are both intergovernmental and horizontal strategies that continue to arise when assessing developmental strategies from below. These parallel strategies found across States, moreover, have seemingly expanded in the face of globalisation and democratisation, sometimes even in contradiction to national policy regimes.

In this sense, it is worth stressing that the "development space" (Naqvi, Henow, & Chang, 2018; Wade, 2003) or "development policy space" (Kentikelenis, Stubbs, & King, 2016) available for subnational governments merits analytical studies, as has been the case thus far for national governments within a globalised context. Kentikelenis et al. (2016) define "policy space as a government's ability to select the policy instruments via which they address their economic problems, free from coercive conditionalities" (p. 547). In an international context, developing countries' strategies, such as those devised by Brazil, India or Mexico, have been constrained to a varying degree in accordance with predicaments laid down by international financial organisations and multilateral frameworks – a feature that has similarly trickled down to subnational platforms with the added constraints inherent to national government prerogatives.

The interscalar dynamics of developmentalism: between compatibility and incompatibility

At the start of the 21st century, Wade (2003) highlighted how "the 'development space' for diversification and upgrading policies in developing countries is being shrunk behind the rhetorical commitment to universal liberalization and privatisation" (p. 622). In a national context, as highlighted by studies cited in previous chapters (Eaton, 2017; Montero, 2002), this "shrinkage" of development space following market-oriented paradigms became one of the factors pushing subnational governments to devise their own regimes or models of industrial policies. Subnational governments, however, have had their "development space" or "development policy space" constrained not only by normative prescriptions (such as multilateral treaties like the TRIPS Agreement or nationally exclusive policies), but also by their dependence on federal resources.

It is thus evident that to be able to enhance their developmental opportunities, subnational governments need to exploit their access to national resources and priorities. Prior to the multilevel conjuncture, subnational governments in authoritarian Mexico were mostly bound to follow the ISI paradigm established at a national level in a compatible interaction between national and subnational policy models. After the multilevel conjuncture, however, subnational governments found themselves needing to redraw more statist-oriented policies even when they contrasted or were incompatible with the national policy regime.

In his study of Asturias' development, Montero (2002) was already tapping into this surging phenomenon. According to his analysis, there was a time in Spain in which national and subnational governments followed different policy regimes or devised "a two tiered strategy of industrial adjustment": at the national level "a policy of reconversion following broad neoliberal principles" and at the subnational level "a strategy of selective intervention based on local politics and the overarching process of decentralizing policy responsibilities and fiscal resources to the regions"

(Montero, 2002, p. 57). This "two-tiered strategy" was in turn reflected in Montero's other subnational developmental case study, Minas Gerais, where the subnational government, along with its developmental technocracy and agencies, devised a more proactive industrial policy in contrast to President Cardoso's neoliberal policies at the turn of the century.

One of the main findings that this study has distilled is thus the emergence of this interscalar incompatibility between economic policy regimes after the multilevel conjuncture witnessed in the previous decades. That does not imply, nevertheless, that subnational governments' responses to national strategies of industrialisation were irrelevant prior to liberal structural reforms across States. As Sinha (2005) pointed out, the prevalence of authoritarian regimes during the second half of the 20th century seems to be an explanative factor for the absence of any meaningful deviations from subnational governments in regards to political economic regimes in States as diverse as China, Brazil, the former Soviet Union and India.

These findings thus echo the case study of Querétaro. In order for Querétaro to overcome its economic backwardness, it had to escalate its subnational industrialisation strategies to fit the national government's industrial and infrastructural priorities, though following closely the same objectives of import substitution and industrial licences or permits. It was only after Mexico's liberalisation that we see instances such as Querétaro and Nuevo León, which were led to formulate proactive industrial policies in contrast to the more market-oriented approach of the federal government.

As highlighted by several scholars on Latin America's development (Panizza, 2009; Grugel & Riggirozzi, 2009), Mexico was one of the region's States that embraced a more radical liberalisation of its economy. And this so-called neoliberal shift, along with the bitter memories of inflation and economic crises during the ISI period, led the Mexican government to retreat from its traditional guidance of economic development or industrial policies (Trejo, 2017; Moreno-Brid, 2013) – generating a policy vacuum which subnational governments such as Querétaro and Nuevo León filled with interesting results. Still, in order for states with developmental potential like Querétaro and Nuevo León to achieve their industrialisation commitments, they found it necessary to integrate their strategies with resources and/or strategies encountered at the national level.

The recent multilevel conjuncture, however, has had its own examples of shortfalls or perils in regards to the devolution of attributions and economic resources within developing countries. After the third wave of democratisation, the instances of "subnational authoritarianism" (Gibson, 2012) or "illiberal structures and practices" (Behrend & Whitehead, 2016) within electoral democracies have evidenced how some subnational governments have extended non-democratic institutions, either formal or informal, despite nationwide tendencies towards democratisation in countries such as Argentina, the United States, Mexico, India, Russia and Brazil.

In the case of Mexico, these practices have had a considerable impact at the subnational level as clientelist mechanisms have balked the developmental potential of states that have undergone a considerable deindustrialisation (such as Estado de Mexico) or states that have wasted opportunities to exploit their geographical advantages (such as the northern state of Coahuila) (see Nichter & Palmer-Rubin, 2014; Freidenberg, 2017, respectively).

In parallel, the devolution of fiscal resources has also given way to negative examples of mismanagement. In Brazil, the unprecedented decentralisation of fiscal resources through the 1988 constitution contributed to severe fiscal crises across numerous states, eventually leading to a recentralising movement during the presidential administration of Fernando Henrique Cardoso (Dillinger, Perry, & Webb, 1999, p. 95). In the words of Montero (2002), "the states in Brazil still reflect both innovative and perverse sides to the decentralization of economic policy-making" (p. 50). Similarly, in Mexico, the unprecedented devolution of fiscal resources during the presidential administration of President Fox (2000–2006) led to an exponential increase in states' debts. During the 1990s, Mexican states had an average debt of 2% of GDP due to hard budget constraints formulated by congress and supervised by the Financial Ministry ("ex ante controls") (Dillinger et al., 1999, p. 98). By the first quarter of 2015, however, the balance of the debt of the states and municipalities as a whole amounted to 510,030.8 million pesos, representing a real growth of 343% between 1993 and 2015 (IMCO, 2015).

Now, after exploring some of the negative notes of decentralisation across developing countries, the following section will summarise the findings of this research regarding partisan factors and their impact on the success or failure of the vertical integration strategies analysed throughout the previous chapters.

Politics as usual? Partisan affinity and intergovernmental dynamics

In the present study, decentralisation and intergovernmental dynamics proved to be a determining factor in subnational governments' possibilities of consolidating a developmental policy regime. The comparative literature on Latin America's decentralisation has stressed thus far the importance of electoral factors, partisan mechanisms and functional criteria when assessing the extent of decentralisation and recentralisation (Willis, Garman & Haggard, 1999; Montero, 2001a; Falleti, 2010). In the specific field of Mexico's industrial policy, the decentralisation of resources and attributions has been similarly affected by political criteria, although within two already different scenarios. Prior to structural liberalisation, Mexico's characteristic centralisation led by its PRI regime required constant efforts of vertical integration even though there was little room for political party divergence. Following its multilevel conjuncture, political factors have accentuated their own relevance in regards to subnational strategies of industrialisation. Since the turn of the century, the vertical strategies available to subnational governments have been mostly dictated thus far by partisan dynamics.

Montero's (2001a) insights on Latin America's intergovernmental relationships included that when "legislative bodies are controlled by parties in opposition to the executive, congress will seek decentralization to limit the powers of the president" (p. 45). This was precisely the case in Mexico, as the coalition of the PRI and PRD in congress achieved unprecedented decentralisation of financial resources during the presidential administration of President Fox (from the PAN).

In the case of Nuevo León, its PRI Governor José Natividad González, along with other governors from the opposition, used the leverage of having a PRI-led majority in the national congress to unbind the traditional fiscal decentralisation that had prevailed in Mexico for a century. Conversely, during the same presidential administration of President Fox, PAN Governor Francisco Garrido exploited his partisan affinities with the President in order to finance Querétaro's new airport, which became essential for the state's construction of its new competitive advantage: the aeronautic sector.

After the review of these vertical patterns in Mexico's subnational cases, chapter 6 was able to highlight similar vertical strategies in both Brazil's Minas Gerais and India's Gujarat. In the case of Minas Gerais, both before and after its multilevel conjuncture, governors were able to push for higher decentralisation of resources and attributions by leveraging their power with congress; furthermore, the constant integration efforts of *mineiro* officials with the national government led them to attain policy access, to land key industrial projects and, eventually, to become members of national developmental agencies.

In the case of Gujarat, the integration between its subnational agencies and the national government was reflected in higher ratios of investment and a higher percentage of industrial licences being approved during India's "licence-raj" system – the latter reflecting another similarity with Querétaro's integration into Mexico's national industrialisation drive, which was similarly controlled by the Ministry of Industry and Commerce's import licences.

In regards to subnational strategies of vertical integration, however, it is worth stressing a difference between Mexico and Brazil, on the one hand, and India, on the other. In these Latin American countries, the agents or actors personally leading their state's integration into the national agenda and its resources were generally governors, underscoring the prominence that these political figures continue to have in the region's political systems. In India, that country's renowned tradition of a meritocratic bureaucracy has seemingly led to more institutionalised and technocratic vehicles of vertical integration across government levels, though the element of partisan affinity or conflict is also seen as determining the contrasting failures that states like West Bengal experienced (see Sinha, 2005). In the new century, however, we begin to witness a higher institutionalisation and delegation among Mexican subnational governments' developmental agencies, leading to new trends in industrial policy that both scholars and development practitioners have deemed better suited for the current globalised context.

From old industrial policy to new industrial policy

Since the turn of the century, examples from developed and developing countries alike have shown the importance of reconfiguring industrial policies as a response to the challenges posed by the international economy. Either through the evolving developmental role of Germany's development bank (Naqvi et al., 2018), the "hidden developmental state" in the United States (Block, 2008) or the apparition of "productive development policies" in Latin America (Crespi, Fernández-Arias & Stein, 2014), industrial policy has been resurfacing in States' agendas, though with a higher emphasis on public-private collaboration, internationalisation and technological innovation.

The present study has thus attempted to capture the differences between old and new industrial policy in Mexico's industrial development. The time-span covering the case study of Querétaro, both before and after Mexico's trade liberalisation, highlights these contrasts that Mexico's development has had between old and new industrial policy. Throughout the 1960s, the subnational government of Querétaro was able to transform Mexico's national drive towards industrialisation by devising its own incentives to attract national and foreign investment, and by formulating its own programmes of industrial estates, which eventually triggered Querétaro's industrial catching-up. During this period of Mexico's ISI (from the 1940s until the end of the 1970s), the national government's industrialisation push consisted of industrial policies with a heavy rate of state intervention and protection of domestic industries through an array of tariff barriers, subsidies, support to SOEs and sector-specific programmes (Gereffi, 2008; Santarcángelo, Schteingart, & Porta, 2018).

Since the 1980s, the Mexican State has been seen as "rather indisposed to adopt industrial policies" (Schneider, 2013, p. 26) or as using industrial policy merely as "rhetoric" (Moreno-Brid & Ros, 2009, p. 224). But even if the Mexican State had a better disposition towards adopting industrial policy in the new century, the State's ongoing fragmentation would also require a more coherent consolidation of its development institutions and governmental units. Contrastingly, subnational platforms such as Nuevo León and Querétaro have shown a more developed institutional system of effective industrial policy, characterised by evolving legal frameworks and an increasing formalisation of industrial relations and state-business synergies.

Thus, after Mexico's trade liberalisation, the national government's retreat from its previous state-led model of industrialisation contributed, among other factors, to an apparition of "robust industrial policies at the state level" (Devlin & Moguillansky, 2013, p. 14). These industrial policies, however, have contrasted with Mexico's "old industrial policy" by emphasising international competitiveness, institutionalisation of good practices, public-private collaboration, clusters, integration into global value chains, R&D incentives, attraction of productive FDI and human capital training – along the lines of Latin America's new industrial policy (Devlin & Moguillansky, 2013) or productive development policies (Crespi et al., 2014).

In this sense, Naudé's (2010) categorisation of industrial policy, according to its domains and its instruments, was relied upon to diagnose the strategies implemented by the developmental policy regimes of both Querétaro and Nuevo León. In the first aspect of this categorisation, an industrial policy domain considers policy areas which pursue an optimisation of a state's economic development – i.e. scientific innovation, selection of industrial sectors, improvement of technological capabilities, and productivity strategies, among others. In the second category, an industrial policy instrument considers the particular mechanism selected by, in this case, a subnational government in order to fulfil its industrial objectives – i.e. tax breaks, price regulations, exchange rate policy, incentives for FDI, infrastructure and funding for cluster formation, and promotion of public-private collaboration, among others.

The cluster policies, in particular, have contributed in both Nuevo León's and Querétaro's efforts to institutionalise public-private collaboration mechanisms while also promoting economic sectors that have been deemed to have greater spill-over potential. Little by little, likewise, the responsibility of leading each state's economic development has been further delegated to the specific and more technically trained governmental units (secretariats or under-secretariats of economic development), moving away from the traditional protagonist role of governors.

In a comparative note, the higher reliance that current States have on FDI to trigger their economic development has led to a competitive impetus between Mexican states, quite similar to dynamics that have been present in the reviewed cases of Brazil and India. And although a wider technology transfer has yet to crystallise in Mexico within FDI projects, Nuevo León's and Querétaro's continuous efforts to integrate local producers into TNCs' global value chains have begun to show promising results in high-technology sectors such as aeronautics (Tzitzi & Feix, 2015; López & Pérez, 2018).

Conclusion

Both the government of Nuevo León and that of Querétaro knowingly developed practices from East Asian, European and Brazilian regions that had experienced considerable industrial accomplishments: namely, the implementation of industrial parks and public-private collaboration through cluster strategies. These efforts regarding industrial policy seemed thus more attuned to Brazil's "new developmentalism", rather than to Mexico's extended neoliberalism.

Nuevo León's government was emphatic on regaining its industrial edge through public-private collaboration, productive investments and incentives for industry and innovation. In this context, the ongoing institutionalisation of Nuevo León's industrial policy was strengthened through several platforms related to its legal frameworks, public-private councils regarding industrial relations, investments and innovation, and a greater reliance on the Secretariat of Economic Development as the organisation in charge of coordinating these policies.

As in the case of Nuevo León, within the new international context, Querétaro made a considerable deviation from the federal government's more market-led policies. It gradually pursued an industrial policy agenda based on public-private collaboration, human capital accumulation, industrial upgrading and the construction of comparative advantages in the subnational state's previously defined strategic sectors. This set of policies was also reminiscent of the "new industrial policies" taking shape in Latin America (Crespi et al., 2014), though constrained to subnational attributions, which excludes any macroeconomic policies, such as the implementation of a competitive exchange rate or protectionist tariffs.

Querétaro is yet another example of how the subnational level seems to be the better platform for these public-private collaborations in industrial matters, as reviewed by Schneider (2013, pp. 21–22). Furthermore, these public-private collaborations were highly reminiscent of strategies enhancing industrial transformation in Nordic Europe (Ornston, 2013) and other countries across the globe (Hausmann, Rodrik & Sabel, 2008; Sinha, 2005; Montero, 2002).

Regarding comparative political economy, prior research by Sinha (2005, 2003) and Montero (2002, 2001b) seems well suited to begin elaborating a comparative framework for a multilevel framework applied to industrial development. The present case studies of Mexican subnational governments are an effort to contribute to this multilevel framework. Consolidating a multilevel perspective for industrialisation could provide further explanatory scope without incurring Sartori's (1970) "conceptual misformation", considering the contemporary reconfiguration of the State. Subnational case studies from India (Sinha, 2005) and Brazil (Montero, 2002) support, therefore, the findings with regards to the two Mexican states examined herein. In both cases of industrial transformation within a new globalised context, variables or factors are present which could be considered "necessary", if not "sufficient conditions" for their success (see De Schweinitz, 1964, p. 7). The main variables constitute a multilevel strategy of both vertical integration and horizontal policies, as presented in Table 7.1.

Table 7.1 Multilevel industrialisation in Nuevo León and Querétaro

	Nuevo León	**Querétaro**
Vertical integration	Fiscal decentralisation of oil-related profits	Financial support in the construction of Querétaro's new airport
	Cooperation with federal government in order to land FDI in Nuevo León's strategic sectors	Securing presidential support regarding Bombardier's investment in Mexico
Horizontal strategies	Cluster or triple-helix strategies	Cluster or triple-helix strategies
	Definition of strategic industrial sectors	Definition of strategic industrial sectors
	Hecho en Nuevo León (Made in Nuevo León) programme with export orientation	Long-term programme for industrial upscaling
	Construction of PIIT to host defined high-tech sectors	Construction of Aeronautic Industrial Park within the airport's premises
	Fiscal and land incentives to promote productive investments	Fiscal and land incentives to promote productive investments
	Secretariat of Economic Development as pilot agency	Under-Secretariat of Economic Development as pilot agency

Source: Author's elaboration.

Though not in the developmental literature's mainstream, there have already been some case studies highlighting subnational efforts towards industrial transformation. However, these case studies which were cited in their majority within previous sections have focused on disaggregating the multilevel characteristics that developmental states have had throughout their history, with an emphasis on the second half of the 20th century. Therefore, one of the central arguments of the present book is that the spatial reconfigurations of the contemporary State, due to the new century's expansion of globalisation, will increasingly diffuse developmental attributes across different State levels. As a consequence, there seems to be a growing gap in the developmental literature that could very well be covered by a multilevel perspective of industrial policy.

In this order of ideas, this research on two Mexican states aimed to contribute precisely to the aforementioned gap, taking into account the increasingly globalised context that the State and its different levels have to face nowadays. As a starting point for future studies, the comparative insight gained by this book's case studies is that a multilevel framework of industrial development should be based on two main variables: firstly, a vertical interaction with the national government, and secondly, a horizontal strategy with an emphasis on institutionalising industrial policy at a subnational level. As noted in the previous sections, these two variables were present, though in different degrees, in the successful cases of subnational industrialisation – be it Minas Gerais, Gujarat, Nuevo León or Querétaro. In conclusion, assessing the multilevel reconfiguration of States could represent a stepping stone in expanding the explanatory scope of industrial policy in future research.

References

Behrend, J., & Whitehead, L. (Eds.). (2016). *Illiberal practices: Territorial variance within large federal democracies*. Baltimore, MD: John Hopkins University Press.

Block, F. (2008). Swimming against the current: The rise of a hidden developmental state in the United States. *Politics & Society, 36*(2), 169–206.

Crespi, G., Fernández-Arias, E., & Stein, E. (Eds.). (2014). *Rethinking productive development*. New York, NY: Palgrave Macmillan.

De Schweinitz, K. (1964). *Industrialization and democracy: Economic necessities and political possibilities*. New York, NY: Free Press.

Devlin, R., & Moguillansky, G. (2013). What's new in the new industrial policy in Latin America? In *The industrial policy revolution I* (pp. 276–317). London: Palgrave Macmillan.

Dillinger, W., Perry, G., & Webb, S. B. (1999). *Macroeconomic management in decentralized democracies: The quest for hard budget constraint in Latin America*. Washington, DC: World Bank.

Eaton, K. (2017). *Territory and ideology in Latin America: Policy conflicts between national and subnational governments*. Oxford: Oxford University Press.

Falleti, T. G. (2010). *Decentralization and subnational politics in Latin America*. Cambridge, UK: Cambridge University Press.

Freidenberg, F. (2017). La otra representación: vínculos clientelares a nivel local en México. *Andamios, 14*(34), 231–258.

Gereffi, G. (2008). Development models and industrial upgrading in China and Mexico. *European Sociological Review, 25*(1), 37–51.

Gibson, E. L. (2012). *Boundary Control: Subnational Authoritarianism in Federal Democracies*. Cambridge: Cambridge University Press.

Grugel, J., & Riggirozzi, P. (2009). The end of the embrace? Neoliberalism and alternatives to neoliberalism in Latin America. In J. Grugel & P. Riggirozzi (Eds.), *Governance after neoliberalism in Latin America* (pp. 1–23). New York, NY: Palgrave Macmillan.

Hausmann, R., Rodrik, D., & Sabel, C. (2008). *Reconfiguring industrial policy: A framework with an application to South Africa*. Cambridge, MA: Harvard University.

Instituto Mexicano para la Competitividad (IMCO) (2015). Reporte Deuda Subnacional. [Online]. Retrieved February 11, 2019, from https://imco.org.mx/wp-content/uploads/2015/07/2015_Reporte_Deuda_subnacional.pdf

Kentikelenis, A. E., Stubbs, T. H., & King, L. P. (2016). IMF conditionality and development policy space, 1985–2014. *Review of International Political Economy, 23*(4), 543–582.

López, M., & Pérez, S. (2018). Los Clústeres como Estrategia de Competitividad en la Industria Aeroespacial en México. In *Innovación y Competitividad en Sectores Estratégicos*. Acapulco: Universidad Autónoma de Guerrero.

Montero, A. P. (2001a). After decentralization: Patterns of intergovernmental conflict in Argentina, Brazil, Spain, and Mexico. *Publius: The Journal of Federalism, 31*(4), 43–64.

Montero, A. P. (2001b). Making and remaking "good government" in Brazil: Subnational industrial policy in Minos Gerais. *Latin American Politics and Society, 43*(2), 49–80.

Montero, A. P. (2002). *Shifting states in global markets: Subnational industrial policy in contemporary Brazil and Spain*. University Park, PA: Penn State University Press.

Moreno-Brid, J., & Ros, J. (2009). *Development and growth in the Mexican economy: A historical perspective*. New York, NY: Oxford University Press.

Moreno-Brid, J. C. (2013). Industrial policy: A missing link in Mexico's quest for export-led growth. *Latin American Policy, 4*(2), 216–237.

Naqvi, N., Henow, A., & Chang, H. J. (2018). Kicking away the financial ladder? German development banking under economic globalisation. *Review of International Political Economy, 25*(5), 672–698.

Naudé, W. (2010). *Industrial policy: Old and new issues (No. 2010, 106)*. Working paper//World Institute for Development Economics Research.

Nichter, S., & Palmer-Rubin, B. (2014). Clientelism, declared support and Mexico's 2012 campaign. In J. I. Domínguez, K. F. Greene, C. H. Lawson, & A. Moreno (Eds.), *Mexico's evolving democracy: A comparative study of the 2012 elections* (pp. 200–226). Baltimore, MD: John Hopkins University Press.

Ornston, D. (2013). Creative corporatism: The politics of high-technology competition in Nordic Europe. *Comparative Political Studies*, *46*(6), 702–729. Retrieved from www.scopus.com/inward/record.url?eid=2-s2.0-84866754935&partnerID= 40&md5=7637a5431243000d8b81bbaa04252f3a

Panizza, F. (2009). *Contemporary Latin America: Development and democracy beyond the Washington consensus*. London: Zed Books Ltd.

Santarcángelo, J. E., Schteingart, D., & Porta, F. (2018). Industrial policy in Argentina, Brazil, Chile and Mexico: A comparative approach. *Revue Interventions économiques. Papers in Political Economy*, (59).

Sartori, G. (1970). Concept misformation in comparative politics. *American Political Science Review*, *64*(4), 1033–1053.

Schneider, B. R. (2013). *Institutions for effective business-government collaboration: Micro mechanisms and macro politics in Latin America*. IDB Working Papers. Washington, DC: Inter-American Development Bank.

Sinha, A. (2003). Rethinking the developmental state model: Divided leviathan and subnational comparisons in India. *Comparative Politics*, 459–476.

Sinha, A. (2005). *The regional roots of developmental politics in India: A divided leviathan*. Indiana: Indiana University Press.

Trejo, A. (2017). Crecimiento económico e industrialización en la Agenda 2030: Perspectivas para México. *Problemas del Desarrollo. Revista Latinoamericana de Economía*, *46*(188).

Tzitzi, M., & Feix, N. (2015). Cómo entender el despegue de Querétaro. *Factor Trabajo BID*. [Online]. Retrieved February 11, 2019, from https://blogs.iadb.org/trabajo/es/como-entender-el-despegue-de-queretaro-en-el-sector-aeroespacial/

Wade, R. H. (2003). What strategies are viable for developing countries today? The World Trade Organization and the shrinking of 'development space'. *Review of International Political Economy*, *10*(4), 621–644.

Willis, E., Garman, C., & Haggard, S. (1999). The politics of decentralization in Latin America. *Latin American Research Review*, 7–56.

Appendix

List of interviews

Sergio Almeida, former delegate in Querétaro of the federal Secretariat of Economy, 23 February 2015.

Ricardo Apaez, Director of the Committee of Innovation of Nuevo León's Automotive Cluster (CLAUT), 7 January 2015.

Jorge Arrambide, former Secretary of Economic Development in Nuevo León (SEDEC), 16 January 2015.

Ramiro Ayala, Regional Director of BANCOMEXT (Mexico's National Bank of International Trade), Monterrey, 2 February 2017.

Cecilia Bustamante, Director of SMEs (Small and Medium Enterprises) in Querétaro's Secretariat of Sustainable Development (SEDESU), 23 February 2015.

Jesús Cantú Escalante, Chairman of Oxfam Mexico's Directive Council, Monterrey, 12 June 2016.

Diego Cárdenas, former PRI Administrative Coordinator in National Congress, Mexico, 5 October 2018.

Alba Luz Cerdán, former coordinator, Programme Hecho en Nuevo León (Made in Nuevo León), Monterrey, 19 January 2015.

Félix Coronado, former delegate in Nuevo León, National Institute for the Social Economy (INAES), Monterrey, 20 January 2015.

Alain Duthoy, adviser, National Action Party (PAN) in National Congress, Mexico, 20 September 2015.

Lorena de la Garza, former Director of Nuevo León's Corporation of Touristic Development (CODEFRONT), Government of Nuevo León, Monterrey, 7 October 2015.

Nayelli Garza, Coordinator of Foreign Investment/European Desk in Secretariat of Economy and Employment of Nuevo León (previously SEDEC), Monterrey, 27 August 2018.

Juan Ramiro Garza Quintanilla, Coordinator of Executive Office in the Government of Nuevo León, Monterrey, 10 June 2018.

Oliver Guajardo, former Director of Querétaro's Airport, Querétaro, 23 February 2015.

Daniel Hernández, Director of Supply Chains in SEDESU, Querétaro, 19 February 2015.

José Luis Huici, former Vice-President of Querétaro's Chamber of the Transformative Industry, Querétaro, 19 February 2015.

Juan Carlos Ituarte, former Under-Secretary of Economic Development in SEDESU, Querétaro, 18 February 2015.

Hugo Mandujano, former Director of Industrial Promotion in SEDESU, phone interview, 10 February 2015.

Enrique Martínez y Martínez, former delegate in Nuevo León of the federal Secretariat of Economy, Monterrey, 20 January 2015.

Mario Mendivil, Coordinator of the Centre of Entrepreneurial Assistance of Nuevo León, Monterrey, 19 January 2015.

Leslie Najera Robledo, Coordinator of the Direction of Industrial Clusters (*Agrupamientos Industriales*) in SEDEC, Monterrey, 15 January 2015.

Artemio Salinas, Vice-President of Global Affairs in Cemex, Monterrey, 5 September 2017.

Héctor Tijerina, former Coordinator for Investments in SEDEC (2015); Director of Investment in Secretariat of Economy and Employment (previously SEDEC) (2018), Monterrey, 14 January 2015 and 27 August 2018.

Rodrigo Villagrán, Coordinator of Investments in SEDESU, Querétaro, 18 February 2015.

Amado Villarreal, researcher in Tec de Monterrey/collaborator with federal Secretariat of Economy, Monterrey, 12 June 2015.

Rolando Zubirán, former Secretary of Economic Development in Nuevo León (SEDEC), Monterrey, 22 January 2015.

Index

Note: Page numbers in *italics* indicate figures, and page numbers **bold** indicate tables on the corresponding pages.

Printed in the United States
by Baker & Taylor Publisher Services